WHATEVER HAPPENED TO WORSHIP?

Whatever Happened to Worship?

Including
*Worship: The Missing Jewel
in the Evangelical Church*

A.W. Tozer

Compiled and edited by Gerald B. Smith

WingSpread Publishers
Chicago, Illinois

WingSpread Publishers
Chicago, Illinois

An imprint of Moody Publishers

Whatever Happened to Worship?
Including *Worship: The Missing Jewel in the Evangelical Church*
ISBN: 978-1-60066-323-9
LOC Control Number: 2011945004
© 1985, 2012 by Christian Publications

Previously published by Christian Publications, Inc.
First Christian Publications Edition 1985
First WingSpread Publishers Edition 2006
Revised WingSpread Publishers Edition 2012

7   9   10   8

Scripture taken from
The Holy Bible: King James Version

Contents

✳

INTRODUCTION

Prior to his death in 1963, Dr. A.W. Tozer expressed the opinion that "worship acceptable to God is the missing crown jewel in evangelical Christianity." He desired to write one more book—a book concerning attitudes in Christian worship.

In 1962, he preached a series of messages, "Worship: The Chief End of Man," from his own pulpit at Avenue Road Church in Toronto. In one of those messages, he told his congregation:

> The coming of the Lord is drawing nigh. I try to do all of my preaching with this in mind. Whatever writing I do is with this possibility in mind.
>
> I want to write one more book on the theme of the worship of God. If I do not succeed in writing that book, it will be all right. I would rather have Jesus Christ come than to write the book.
>
> I have read that John Wesley was asked at one time how he would react if he knew that Christ was coming that very night. His instant reply was, "I don't think I would change any of my plans."

Gerald B. Smith took great care in compiling, arranging and editing those sermons so that Dr. Tozer's concerns come forth clearly, even as he spoke them in 1962. The themes he preached more than twenty years ago seem timely yet, and his appeals are even more urgent than they were at that time.

In this new edition of *Whatever Happened to Worship?*,

WingSpread Publishers has included another popular sermon series: "Worship: The Missing Jewel in the Evangelical Church." These sermons, preached in 1961 to pastors of the Associated Gospel Churches of Canada, have been in print since Tozer himself edited them for the association's publication, *Advance*. In 1965, the articles were published in *The Alliance Witness* (which later became *Alliance Life*), the magazine for which Tozer served as editor from 1950 until his death in 1963 and later in a very popular booklet form.

CHAPTER 1

WORSHIP IN THE CHRISTIAN CHURCH

I know thy works, that thou art neither cold nor hot: I would thou wert cold or hot.

So then because thou art lukewarm, and neither cold nor hot, I will spue thee out of my mouth.

Because thou sayest, I am rich, and increased with goods, and have need of nothing; and knowest not that thou art wretched, and miserable, and poor, and blind, and naked:

I counsel thee to buy of me gold tried in the fire, that thou mayest be rich; and white raiment, that thou mayest be clothed, and that the shame of thy nakedness do not appear; and anoint thine eyes with eyesalve, that thou mayest see.

As many as I love, I rebuke and chasten: be zealous therefore, and repent.

Behold, I stand at the door, and knock: if any man hear my voice, and open the door, I will come in to him, and will sup with him, and he with me.

To him that overcometh will I grant to sit with me in my throne, even as I also overcame, and am set down with my Father in his throne.

He that hath an ear, let him hear what the Spirit saith unto the churches. (Revelation 3:15–22)

Christian churches have come to the dangerous time predicted long ago. It is a time when we can pat one another on the back, congratulate ourselves and join in the glad refrain, "We are rich, and increased with goods, and have need of nothing!"

It certainly is true that hardly anything is missing from our churches these days—except the most important thing. We are missing the genuine and sacred offering of ourselves and our worship to the God and Father of our Lord Jesus Christ.

In the message of the Revelation, the angel of the church of the Laodiceans made this charge and this appeal: "Thou sayest, I am rich, and increased with goods, and have need of nothing.... As many as I love, I rebuke and chasten: be zealous therefore, and repent" (3:17, 19).

My own loyalties and responsibilities are and always will be with the strongly evangelical, Bible-believing, Christ-honoring churches. We have been surging forward. We are building great churches and large congregations. We are boasting about high standards, and we are talking a lot about revival.

But I have a question and it is not just rhetoric: *What has happened to our worship?*

The reply of many is, "We are rich and have need of nothing. Doesn't that say something about God's blessing?"

Did you know that the often-quoted Jean-Paul Sartre describes his turning to philosophy and hopelessness as a turning away from a secularistic church? He says, "I did not recognize in the fashionable God who was taught me,

Him who was waiting for my soul. I needed a Creator; I was given a big businessman!"

None of us is as concerned as we should be about the image we really project to the community around us. At least not when we profess to belong to Jesus Christ and still fail to show forth His love and compassion as we should.

We who are the fundamentalists and the "orthodox" Christians have gained the reputation of being "tigers"—great fighters for the truth. Our hands are heavy with callouses from the brass knuckles we have worn as we beat on the liberals. Because of the meaning of our Christian faith for a lost world, we are obligated to stand up for the truth and to contend for the faith when necessary.

But there is a better way, even in our dealing with those who are liberals in faith and theology. We can do a whole lot more for them by being Christlike than we can by figuratively beating them over the head with our knuckles.

The liberals tell us they cannot believe the Bible. They tell us they cannot believe that Jesus Christ was the unique Son of God. At least most of them are honest about it. Moreover, I am certain we are not going to make them bow the knee by cursing them. If we are led by the Spirit of God and if we show forth the love of God this world needs, we become the "winsome saints."

The strange and wonderful thing about it is that truly winsome and loving saints do not even know about their attractiveness. The great saints of past eras did not know they were great saints. If someone had told them, they would not have believed it, but those around them knew that Jesus was living His life in them.

I think we join the winsome saints when God's purposes in Christ become clear to us. We join them when we begin to worship God because He is who He is.

Sometimes evangelical Christians seem to be fuzzy and uncertain about the nature of God and His purposes in creation and redemption. In such instances, the preachers often are to blame. There are still preachers and teachers who say that Christ died so we would not drink and not smoke and not go to the theater.

No wonder people are confused! No wonder they fall into the habit of backsliding when such things are held up as the reason for salvation.

Jesus was born of a virgin, suffered under Pontius Pilate, died on the cross and rose from the grave to make worshippers out of rebels! He has done it all through grace. We are the recipients.

That may not sound dramatic, but it is God's revelation and God's way.

Another example of our wrong thinking about God is the attitude of so many that God is now a charity case. He is a kind of frustrated foreman who cannot find enough help. He stands at the wayside asking how many will come to His rescue and begin to do His work.

Oh, if we would only remember who He is! God has never actually needed any of us—not one. But we pretend that He does, and we make it a big thing when someone agrees "to work for the Lord."

We all should be willing to work for the Lord, but it is a matter of grace on God's part. I am of the opinion that we should not be concerned about working for God until we have learned the meaning and the delight of worshipping Him.

A worshipper can work with eternal quality in his work. But a worker who does not worship is only piling up wood, hay and stubble for the time when God sets the world on fire (see 1 Corinthians 3:10–15).

I fear that there are many professing Christians who do not want to hear such statements about their "busy schedule," but it is the truth. God is trying to call us back to that for which He created us—to worship Him and to enjoy Him forever!

It is then, out of our deep worship, that we do His work.

I heard a college president say that the church is "suffering from a rash of amateurism."

Any untrained, unprepared, unspiritual empty rattle-trap of a person can start something religious and find plenty of followers who will listen and pay and promote it. It might become very evident that he or she had never heard from God in the first place.

These things are happening all around us because we are not worshippers. If we are truly among the worshippers, we will not be spending our time with carnal or worldly religious projects.

All of the examples that we have in the Bible illustrate that glad and devoted and reverent worship is the normal employment of moral beings. Every glimpse that is given us of heaven and of God's created beings is always a glimpse of worship and rejoicing and praise because God is who He is. The Apostle John in Revelation 4:10–11 gives us a plain portrayal of created beings around the throne of God. John speaks of the occupation of the elders in this way:

> The four and twenty elders fall down before him that sat on the throne, and worship him that liveth for ever and ever, and cast their crowns before the throne, saying,
>
> Thou art worthy, O Lord, to receive glory and honour

and power: for thou hast created all things, and for thy
pleasure they are and were created.

I can safely say, on the authority of all that is revealed
in the Word of God, that any man or woman on this earth
who is bored and turned off by worship is not ready for
heaven.

But I can almost hear someone saying, "Is Tozer getting away from justification by faith? Haven't we always
heard that we are justified and saved and on our way to
heaven by faith?"

I assure you that Martin Luther never believed in justification by faith more strongly than I do. I believe in
justification by faith. I believe we are saved by having
faith in the Son of God as Lord and Savior. But nowadays
there is a deadly, automatic quality about getting saved. It
bothers me greatly.

I say an "automatic" quality: "Put a nickel's worth of
faith in the slot, pull down the lever and take out the little
card of salvation. Tuck it in your wallet and off you go!"

After that, the man or woman can say, "Yes, I'm saved."
How does he or she know?

"I put the nickel in. I accepted Jesus, and I signed the
card."

Very good. There is nothing intrinsically wrong with
signing a card. It can be a helpful thing so we know who
has made inquiry.

But really, my brother or sister, we are brought to God
and to faith and to salvation that we might worship and
adore Him. We do not come to God that we might be automatic Christians, cookie-cutter Christians, Christians
stamped out with a die.

God has provided His salvation that we might be, individually and personally, vibrant children of God, loving God with all our hearts and worshipping Him "in the beauty of holiness" (Psalm 29:2).

This does not mean, and I am not saying, that we must all worship alike. The Holy Spirit does not operate by anyone's preconceived idea or formula. But this I know: When the Holy Spirit of God comes among us with His anointing, we become a worshipping people. This may be hard for some to admit, but when we are truly worshipping and adoring the God of all grace and of all love and of all mercy and of all truth, we may not be quiet enough to please everyone.

I recall Luke's description of the throngs on that first Palm Sunday:

> The whole multitude of the disciples began to rejoice and praise God with a loud voice for all the mighty works that they had seen;
>
> Saying, Blessed be the King that cometh in the name of the Lord: peace in heaven, and glory in the highest.
>
> And some of the Pharisees from among the multitude said unto him, Master, rebuke thy disciples.
>
> And he answered and said unto them, I tell you that, if these should hold their peace, the stones would immediately cry out. (Luke 19:37–40)

Let me say two things here.

First, I do not believe it is necessarily true that we are worshipping God when we are making a lot of racket. But not infrequently worship is audible.

When Jesus came into Jerusalem presenting Himself as Messiah, there was a great multitude and there was a great noise. Doubtless many who joined in the singing and the praise had never been able to sing in the right key. When you have a group of people singing anywhere, you know that some of them will not be in tune.

But this is the point to their worship: They were united in praises to God.

Second, I would warn those who are cultured, quiet, self-possessed, poised and sophisticated, that if they are embarrassed in church when some happy Christian says "Amen!" they may actually be in need of some spiritual enlightenment. The worshipping saints of God in the body of Christ have often been a little bit noisy. I hope you have read some of the devotionals left us by that dear old English saint Lady Julian, who lived more than six hundred years ago.

She wrote that one day she had been thinking about how high and lofty Jesus was, and yet how He Himself meets the humblest part of our human desire. She received such blessing within her being that she could not control herself. She let go with a shout and praised God out loud in Latin.

Translated into English, it would have come out, "Well, glory to God!"

Now, if that bothers you, friend, it might be because you do not know the kind of spiritual blessings and delight the Holy Spirit is waiting to provide among God's worshipping saints.

Did you notice what Luke said about the Pharisees and their request that Jesus should rebuke His disciples for praising God with loud voices? Their ritual rules probably allowed them to whisper the words, "Glory to God!," but it really pained them to hear anyone saying them out loud.

Jesus told the Pharisees in effect: "They are doing the right thing. God my Father and I and the Holy Ghost are to be worshipped. If men and women will not worship me, the very rocks will shout my praises!"

Those religious Pharisees, polished and smoothed and polished again, would have died right there in their tracks if they had heard a rock given a voice and praising the Lord.

Well, we have great churches and we have beautiful sanctuaries and we join in the chorus, "We have need of nothing." But there is every indication that we are in need of worshippers.

We have a lot of men willing to sit on our church boards who have no desire for spiritual joy and radiance and who never show up for the church prayer meeting. These are the men who often make the decisions about the church budget and the church expenses and where the frills will go in the new edifice.

They are the fellows who run the church, but you cannot get them to the prayer meeting because they are not worshippers.

Perhaps you do not think this is an important matter, but that puts you on the other side as far as I am concerned.

It seems to me that it has always been a frightful incongruity that men who do not pray and do not worship are nevertheless actually running many of the churches and ultimately determining the direction they will take.

It hits very close to our own situations, perhaps, but we should confess that in many "good" churches, we let the women do the praying and let the men do the voting.

Because we are not truly worshippers, we spend a lot of time in the churches just spinning our wheels, burning the gasoline, making a noise but not getting anywhere.

Oh, brother or sister, God calls us to worship, but in

many instances we are in entertainment, just running a poor second to the theaters.

That is where we are, even in the evangelical churches, and I don't mind telling you that most of the people we say we are trying to reach will never come to a church to see a lot of amateur actors putting on a home talent show.

I tell you, outside of politics there is not another field of activity that has more words and fewer deeds, more wind and less rain.

What are we going to do about this awesome, beautiful worship that God calls for? I would rather worship God than do any other thing I know of in all this wide world.

I would not even attempt to tell you how many hymnbooks are piled up in my study. I cannot sing a lick, but that is nobody's business. God thinks I am an opera star! God listens while I sing to Him the old French hymns in translation, the old Latin hymns in translation. God listens while I sing the old Greek hymns from the Eastern church as well as the beautiful psalms done in meter and some of the simpler songs of Watts and Wesley and the rest.

I mean it when I say that I would rather worship God than to do anything else. You may reply, "If you worship God, you do nothing else."

But that only reveals that you have not done your homework. The beautiful part of worship is that it prepares you and enables you to zero in on the important things that must be done for God.

Listen to me! Practically every great deed done in the church of Christ all the way back to the Apostle Paul was done by people blazing with the radiant worship of their God.

A survey of church history will prove that it was those

who were the yearning worshippers who also became the great workers. Those great saints whose hymns we so tenderly sing were active in their faith to the point that we must wonder how they ever did it all.

The great hospitals have grown out of the hearts of worshipping men. The mental institutions grew out of the hearts of worshipping and compassionate men and women. We should say too that wherever the church has come out of her lethargy, rising from her sleep and into the tides of revival and spiritual renewal, always the worshippers were back of it.

We will be making a mistake if we just stand back and say, "But if we give ourselves to worship, no one will do anything."

On the contrary, if we give ourselves to God's call to worship, everyone will do more than he or she is doing now. Only, what he or she does will have significance and meaning to it. It will have the quality of eternity in it—it will be gold, silver and precious stones, not wood, hay and stubble (see 1 Corinthians 3:10–15).

Why should we be silent about the wonders of God? We should gladly join Isaac Watts in one of his worship hymns:

Bless, O my soul, the living God,
Call home thy thoughts that roam abroad,

That all the powers within me join
In work and worship so divine.

Bless, O my soul, the God of grace,
His favors claim thy highest praise.

Why should the wonders He has wrought
Be lost in silence, and forgot?

Let the whole earth His power confess,

Let the whole earth adore His grace.
The Gentiles, with the Jews, shall join
In work and worship so divine.

I cannot speak for you, but I want to be among those who worship. I do not want just to be a part of some great ecclesiastical machine where the pastor turns the crank and the machine runs. You know—the pastor loves everybody and everybody loves him. He has to do it. He is paid to do it.

I wish that we might get back to worship again. Then when people come into the church, they will instantly sense that they have come among holy people, God's people. They can testify, "Of a truth God is in this place."

Chapter 2

True Worship Demands the New Birth

And you hath he quickened, who were dead in trespasses and sins;

Wherein in time past ye walked according to the course of this world, according to the prince of the power of the air, the spirit that now worketh in the children of disobedience:

Among whom also we all had our conversation in times past in the lusts of our flesh, fulfilling the desires of the flesh and of the mind; and were by nature the children of wrath, even as others.

But God, who is rich in mercy, for his great love wherewith he loved us,

Even when we were dead in sins, hath quickened us together with Christ, (by grace ye are saved;)

And hath raised us up together, and made us sit together in heavenly places in Christ Jesus:

That in the ages to come he might shew the exceeding riches of his grace in his kindness toward us through Christ Jesus.

For by grace are ye saved through faith; and that not of yourselves: it is the gift of God:

Not of works, lest any man should boast.

For we are his workmanship, created in Christ Jesus unto good works, which God hath before ordained that we should walk in them. (Ephesians 2:1–10)

There are many weird ideas about God in our day, and therefore there are all kinds of substitutes for true worship.

Often I have heard someone or another within the Christian church confess sadly: "I guess I don't really know very much about God."

If that is a true confession, the man or woman should then be honest enough to make a necessarily parallel confession: "I guess I don't really know very much about worship."

Actually, basic beliefs about the person and the nature of God have changed so much that there are among us now men and women who find it easy to brag about the benefits they receive from God—without ever a thought or a desire to know the true meaning of worship!

I have immediate reactions to such an extreme mis-understanding of the true nature of a holy and sovereign God.

My first is that I believe the very last thing God desires is to have shallow-minded and worldly Christians brag-ging about Him.

My second is that it does not seem to be very well recognized that God's highest desire is that every one of His believing children should so love and so adore Him that we are continuously in His presence, in Spirit and in truth.

That is to worship, indeed.

Something wonderful and miraculous and life-changing takes place within the human soul when Jesus

Christ is invited in to take His rightful place. That is exactly what God anticipated when He wrought the plan of salvation. He intended to make worshippers out of rebels; He intended to restore to men and women the place of worship which our first parents knew when they were created.

If we know this result as a blessed reality in our own lives and experience, then it is evident that we are not just waiting for Sunday to come so we can "go to church and worship."

True worship of God must be a constant and consistent attitude or state of mind within the believer. It will always be a sustained and blessed acknowledgment of love and adoration, subject in this life to degrees of perfection and intensity.

Now, the negative side of the common approach to worship needs to be stated. Contrary to much that is being said and practiced in the churches, true worship of God is not something that we "do" in the hope of appearing to be religious!

No one can really argue that many people whose dearest desire is just to be numbered with those who are "sensitive to religion" place their weekly emphasis upon faithfulness in attending "the service of worship."

What do the Christian Scriptures have to say to us at this point as we consider the reality of fellowship between God and His redeemed children? What we learn is very plain and very encouraging. Having been made in His image, we have within us the capacity to know God and the instinct that we should worship Him. The very moment that the Spirit of God has quickened us to His life in regeneration, our whole being senses its kinship to God and leaps up in joyous recognition!

That response within our beings, a response to forgiveness and pardon and regeneration, signals the miracle of the heavenly birth—without which we cannot see the kingdom of God.

Yes, God desires and is pleased to communicate with us through the avenues of our minds, our wills and our emotions. The continuous and unembarrassed interchange of love and thought between God and the souls of redeemed men and women is the throbbing heart of the New Testament religion.

Actually, it is impossible to consider this new relationship without confessing that the primary work of the Holy Spirit is to restore the lost soul to intimate fellowship with God through the washing of regeneration.

To accomplish this, He first reveals Christ to the penitent heart: "Wherefore I give you to understand, that no man speaking by the Spirit of God calleth Jesus accursed: and that no man can say that Jesus is the Lord, but by the Holy Ghost" (1 Corinthians 12:3).

Then consider Christ's own words to His disciples concerning the brighter rays from His own being which will illuminate the newborn soul:

"But the Comforter, which is the Holy Ghost, whom the Father will send in my name, he shall teach you all things, and bring all things to your remembrance, whatsoever I have said unto you" (John 14:26).

Remember, we know Christ only as the Spirit enables us. How thankful we should be to discover that it is God's desire to lead every willing heart into depths and heights of divine knowledge and communion.

As soon as God sends the Spirit of His Son into our hearts, we say "Abba"—and we are worshipping, but probably not in the full New Testament sense of the word.

God desires to take us deeper into Himself. We will have much to learn in the school of the Spirit.

He wants to lead us on in our love for Him who first loved us. He wants to cultivate within us the adoration and admiration of which He is worthy. He wants to reveal to each of us the blessed element of spiritual fascination in true worship. He wants to teach us the wonder of being filled with moral excitement in our worship, entranced with the knowledge of who God is. He wants us to be astonished at the inconceivable elevation and magnitude and splendor of Almighty God!

There can be no human substitute for this kind of worship and for this kind of Spirit-given response to the God who is our Creator and Redeemer and Lord.

There is all around us, however, a very evident and continuing substitute for worship. I speak of the compelling temptation among Christian believers to be constantly engaged, during every waking hour, in religious activity.

We cannot deny that it is definitely a churchly idea of service. Many of our sermons and much of our contemporary ecclesiastical teaching lean toward the idea that it is surely God's plan for us to be busy, busy, busy—because it is the best cause in the world in which we are involved.

But if there is any honesty left in us, it persuades us in our quieter moments that true spiritual worship is at a discouragingly low ebb among professing Christians.

Do we dare ask how we have reached this state?

If you are willing to ask it, I am willing to try to answer it.

Actually, I will answer it by asking another obvious question. How can our approach to worship be any more vital than it is when so many who lead us, both in the pulpit and in the pew, give little indication that the fellowship of God is delightful beyond telling?

Think back for a moment into your New Testament knowledge, and you will have to agree that this is exactly the point that Jesus was making to the stern and self-righteous Pharisees about true worship in their day.

They were religious in their daily life. They were outwardly pious and well acquainted with the forms of worship—but within their beings were attitudes and faults and hypocrisies that caused Jesus to describe them as "whitewashed sepulchers" (see Matthew 23:27).

The only righteousness they knew and understood was their own outward form of righteousness based on the maintenance of a fairly high level of external morality.

Because they thought of God as being as stern and austere and unforgiving as they themselves were, their concept of worship was necessarily low and unworthy.

To a Pharisee, the service of God was a bondage, which he did not love but from which he could not escape without a loss too great to bear. God, as the Pharisees saw Him, was not a God easy to live with. So their daily religion became grim and hard, with no trace of true love in it.

It can be said about us, as humans, that we try to be like our God. If He is conceived to be stern and exacting and harsh, so will we be!

The blessed and inviting truth is that God is the most winsome of all beings, and in our worship of Him, we should find unspeakable pleasure.

The living God has been willing to reveal Himself to our seeking hearts. He would have us know and understand that He is all love and that those who trust Him need never know anything but that love.

God would have us know that He is just, indeed, and

He will not condone sin. He has tried to make it overwhelmingly plain to us that through the blood of the everlasting covenant, He is able to act toward us exactly as if we had never sinned.

Unbeknown to the understanding of a Pharisee, God communes with His redeemed ones in an easy, uninhibited fellowship that is restful and healing to the soul.

The God who has redeemed us in love, through the merits of the Eternal Son, is not unreasonable. He is not selfish. Neither is He temperamental. What He is today we shall find Him tomorrow and the next day and next year.

The God who desires our fellowship and communion is not hard to please, although He may be hard to satisfy. He expects of us only what He has Himself supplied. He is quick to mark every simple effort to please Him and just as quick to overlook our imperfections when He knows we meant to do His will.

This is the best of good news: God loves us for ourselves. He values our love more than He values galaxies of newly created worlds. He remembers our frame and knows that we are dust (see Psalm 103:14).

The God we love may sometimes chasten us, it is true. But even this He does with a smile—the proud, tender smile of a Father who is bursting with pleasure over an imperfect but promising son who is coming every day to look more and more like the One whose child he is.

We should revel in the joy of believing that God is the sum of all patience and the true essence of kindly goodwill. We please Him most, not by frantically trying to make ourselves good, but by throwing ourselves into His arms with all our imperfections and believing that He understands everything—and loves us still.

The gratifying part of all this is that the intercourse between God and the redeemed soul is known to us in conscious, personal awareness.

It is a personal awareness, indeed. The awareness does not come through the body of believers, as such, but is known to the individual, and to the body through the individuals composing it.

And, yes, it is conscious; it does not stay below the threshold of consciousness and work there unknown to the soul.

This communication, this consciousness is not an end but really an inception. There is the point of reality where we begin our fellowship and friendship and communion with God. But where we stop no man has yet discovered, for there is in the mysterious depths of the triune God neither limit nor end.

When we come into this sweet relationship, we are beginning to learn astonished reverence, breathless adoration, awesome fascination, lofty admiration of the attributes of God and something of the breathless silence that we know when God is near.

You may never have realized it before, but all of those elements in our perception and consciousness of the divine Presence add up to what the Bible calls "the fear of God."

We can know a million fears in our hours of pain or in threats of danger or in the anticipation of punishment or death. What we need to plainly recognize is that the fear of God the Bible commends can never be induced by threats or punishment of any kind.

The fear of God is that "astonished reverence" of which the great Faber wrote. I would say that it may grade anywhere from its basic element—the terror of the guilty soul before a holy God—to the fascinated rapture of the worshipping saint. There are very few unqualified things in our lives, but I believe that the reverential fear of God mixed with love and fascination and astonishment and admiration and devotion is the most enjoyable state and the most purifying emotion the human soul can know.

In my own being I could not exist very long as a Christian without this inner consciousness of the presence and nearness of God.

I guess there are some persons who find themselves strong enough to live day by day on the basis of ethics without any intimate spiritual experience.

They say Benjamin Franklin was such a man. He was a deist and not a Christian. Whitefield prayed for him and told him he was praying for him, but Franklin said, "I guess it is not doing any good because I am not saved yet."

This is what Franklin did. He kept a daily graph on a series of little square charts, which represented such virtues as honesty, faithfulness, charity and probably a dozen others. He worked these into a kind of calendar and when he had violated one of the virtues, he would write it down. When he had gone for a day or a month without having broken any of his self-imposed commandments, he considered that he was doing pretty well as a human being.

A sense of ethics? Yes.

Any sense of the divine? No.

No mystical overtone. No worship. No reverence. No fear of God before his eyes. All of this according to his own testimony.

I do not belong to that breed of man. I can only keep right by keeping the fear of God on my soul and delighting in the fascinated rapture of worship. Apart from that, I do not know any rules at all.

I am sorry that this powerful sense of godly fear is a missing quality in the churches today, and its absence is a portent and a sign.

It should hover over us like the cloud over Israel. It should lie upon us like a sweet, invisible mantle. It should be a force in the conditioning of our inner lives. It should provide extra meaning for every text of Scripture. It should be making every day of the week a holy day and every spot of ground we tread holy ground.

We continue to shake from our own kinds of fears: fear of Communism, fear of the collapse of civilization, even the fear of invasion from some other planet. Men think they know what fear means.

But we are talking about the awe and the reverence of a loving and holy God. That kind of a fear of God is a spiritual thing and can be brought only by the Presence of God.

When the Holy Spirit came at Pentecost, there was a great fear upon all the people, yet they were not afraid of anything! A child of God, made perfect in love, has no fear because perfect love casts out fear. Yet he or she is the person of all persons who most fears God.

Take the Apostle John as an illustration. When Jesus was arrested in the garden, John was among those who ran away. Probably he was afraid of being arrested and put into jail. That was his fear of danger, fear of punishment, fear of humiliation.

But later the same John, exiled on Patmos for the testimony of Jesus Christ, saw an awesome man standing amid the golden lampstands. The man was clothed in a white robe and girded with a golden girdle. His feet were like burnished brass, and a sword proceeded from His mouth. His hair was as white as snow and His face shone like the sun in its strength. The awe and reverence and fascination and fear suddenly concentrated so completely in John's being that he could only fall unconscious to the ground (see Revelation 1:12–17).

Then this holy Priest whom he later found was Jesus Christ Himself, bearing the keys of death and hell, came and lifted John up and brought life back into him.

Now, John was not afraid, and he did not feel threatened. He was experiencing a different kind of fear, a godly fear. It was a holy thing, and John felt it.

The Presence of God in our midst—bringing a sense of godly fear and reverence—this is largely missing today.

You cannot induce it by soft organ music and light streaming through beautifully designed windows. You cannot induce it by holding up a biscuit and claiming that it is God. You cannot induce it by any kind or any amount of mumbo jumbo.

What people feel in the presence of that kind of paganism is not the true fear of God. It is just the inducement of a superstitious dread.

A true fear of God is a beautiful thing, for it is worship, it is love, it is veneration. It is a high moral happiness because God is.

It is a delight so great that if God were not, the worshipper would not want to be, either. He or she could easily pray, "My God, continue to be as Thou art, or let me die! I cannot think of any other God but Thee!"

True worship is to be so personally and hopelessly in love with God that the idea of a transfer of affection never even remotely exists.

That is the meaning of the fear of God.

Because worship is largely missing, do you know what we are doing? We are doing our best to sew up that rent veil in the temple (see Luke 23:45). We use artificial means to try to induce some kind of worship.

I think the devil in hell must be laughing, and I think God must be grieving, for there is no fear of God before our eyes.

CHAPTER 3

MUCH THAT IS CALLED WORSHIP IS NOT

The woman saith unto him, Sir, I perceive that thou art a prophet.

Our fathers worshipped in this mountain; and ye say, that in Jerusalem is the place where men ought to worship.

Jesus saith unto her, Woman, believe me, the hour cometh, when ye shall neither in this mountain, nor yet at Jerusalem, worship the Father.

Ye worship ye know not what: we know what we worship: for salvation is of the Jews.

But the hour cometh, and now is, when the true worshippers shall worship the Father in spirit and in truth: for the Father seeketh such to worship him.

God is a Spirit: and they that worship him must worship him in spirit and in truth. (John 4:19–24)

The whole import and substance of the Bible teaches us that the God who does not need anything nevertheless desires the adoration and worship of His created children.

This conclusion is more than a matter of proof texts. Our Lord Himself said it plainly and with certainty when

He was here upon this earth. "Thou shalt worship the Lord thy God, and him only shalt thou serve" (Luke 4:8).

There is not a tribe in all the world that does not have some kind of religion and some form of worship. Men and women have an instinct toward worship.

I once wrote an editorial in which I pointed out my feeling that when a man falls on his knees and stretches out his hands and says, "Our Father which art in heaven," he is doing what seems natural to him.

One elderly gentlemen, when he read the editorial, took vehement exception to it. He wrote that "only a completely liberal editor" would say that worship is a natural thing with mankind.

The fact is that God made us to worship Him, and if we had not fallen with Adam and Eve, worship would have been the most natural thing for us.

Sinning was not the natural thing for Adam and Eve, but they disobeyed and fell, losing their privilege of perfect fellowship with God, the Creator. Sin is the unnatural thing; it was never intended by God to be in our nature.

The brief summary of this important matter is that God still desires worship, but we must learn that we cannot have our own way and worship God just as we please.

Have you ever given thought to the words of our Lord Jesus Christ when He referred to a certain group of religious people in His own day with the comment: "They worship they know not what"? (see John 4:22).

I dare to tell you that Jesus was actually emphasizing a very cogent truth about worship. It is entirely possible for humans to have recognized forms of worship apart from Christ and apart from the salvation He offers.

I need to go even a little further beyond that statement to point out a similar and parallel truth. Authentic religious experience is altogether possible apart from Christ.

Now, I hope you are not misunderstanding me and charging me in your own mind with heresy.

Yes, I said there may be worship apart from Christ, and I said there may be authentic religious experience apart from Christ.

But I did not say—and I do not believe—that such religious experiences or forms of worship are acceptable to God. There are certain kinds of worship that God will not accept, though they may be directed toward Him and meant to be given to Him.

It is recorded that when Jesus was teaching here on earth, He told His hearers that the day would come when people would say to Him, "Did not we do miracles in Your name? Did not we speak for You on the street corner?"

Do you remember the sternness and the sharpness of His reply? "I never knew you! Depart from Me!" (See Luke 13:26–27; see also Matthew 7:22–24).

Men and women on this earth ought never to fool themselves about the reality of true worship that must always be in spirit and in truth. It is plainly possible to have religious experience and forms of worship that are not at all acceptable to God.

The Apostle Paul wrote something very sharp and plain and final to the early Christian church in Corinth. Paul knew very definitely that men and women could engage in an experience of worship and still not worship according to the will of God. Thus their worship would not be accepted by God at all.

Listen to what Paul declares: "The things which the Gentiles sacrifice, they sacrifice to devils, and not to God: and I would not that ye should have fellowship with devils" (1 Corinthians 10:20).

Paul was surely teaching that every form of idolatry is hated by God. It is hated for the very reason that it is real. Forms of idolatry can become very real to those who engage in them, but that does not make them acceptable to the living God.

That is one of the reasons why Jesus said of a certain group, "They worship they know not what." It is possible to have some of the elements of worship—perhaps admiration, self-abasement, surrender, attachment—and not be among the redeemed at all.

I think it is worthy to note that Thomas Carlyle, in his *On Heroes and Hero-Worship, and the Heroic in History*, warned us not to make the mistake of thinking that the great pagan religions of the world are all phony. Carlyle declared that from his investigation, those great forms of religion are not phony at all. They are real, and the terror of them is that they are real.

Years ago in Mexico, I was attracted by the sight of an old, old church. I walked in with my hat removed and found that the church had no floor except the ground itself.

I paused to look around at the statues and the carvings and then noticed that an elderly Mexican lady had come into the building. She was carrying a small shopping bag.

She paid no attention to me but walked straight down to the altar area. I had the feeling she was so familiar with that aisle she could have walked it with her eyes closed.

She walked directly to kneel in front of a statue of the Virgin Mary. She looked up into the facial features of the inanimate statue with deep devotion, deep yearning, deep desire. I thought, "That is the kind of spiritual longing and desire that I would like to see turned to the Lord Himself!"

There was no doubt in my mind that she was having an experience of worship. I believe it was very real to her. She was not pretending. She wanted to worship, but her worship was being poured out on a lifeless statue, which was only the work of some person's hands.

There are many kinds of worship that God cannot accept. Cain's worship in the Old Testament was not accepted because he did not acknowledge the necessity of an atonement for sin in the relationship between God and fallen man.

Cain hoped to please God in worship, but he brought no blood sacrifice. He came instead with an offering "of the fruit of the ground," probably beautiful flowers and a basket of fruit (see Genesis 4:1–8).

When God frowned on his gift, Cain's attitude and answer seemed to be, "I don't know anything about this sin-and-atonement idea." God's rejection of his offering and His acceptance of Abel's "firstlings of his flock" made Cain so angry that he went out and killed his brother.

The kind of worship Cain offered to God has three basic and serious shortcomings.

First is the mistaken idea that God is a different kind of God than what He really is. This has to do with the person and the character of the sovereign and holy God. How can anyone ever worship God acceptably without knowing what kind of God He really is? Cain surely did not know the true character of God. Cain did not believe that the matter of man's sin was eternally important to God.

Second is the mistake of thinking that man holds a relationship to God that in fact he does not. Cain casually assumed that he was deserving of acceptance by the Lord without any intermediary. He refused to accept the judgment of God that man had been alienated from his God by sin.

Third, Cain in the Old Testament record, and with him an unnumbered multitude of men and women since, have mistakenly assumed that sin is far less serious than it really is. The record is plain, if men and women would only look at it and consider it. God hates sin because He is a holy God. He knows that sin has filled the world with pain and sorrow, robbing us of our principal purpose and joy in life, the joy of worshipping our God!

The kind of worship offered by Cain is inadequate, without real meaning. Bringing it as an issue to our own day under the New Testament, I assure you that I would not knowingly spend an hour in any church that refuses to teach the necessity of the blood atonement for sin through the cross and the merits of the death of our Lord Jesus Christ!

Another kind of unacceptable worship is symbolized by the attitude of the Samaritans in the Bible. The Old Testament history reveals that Jeroboam, the first king of Israel after it became the Northern Kingdom, set up two places of worship. He wanted to be sure his people were weaned from their habit of worshipping at Jerusalem. He installed golden calves to be worshipped in convenient places, Bethel and Dan.

The heresy of Samaritanism—the practice of picking out what we like to worship and rejecting what we do not like—is widespread.

Actually, it has opened up a whole new field for applied psychology and humanism under a variety of religious disguises. In this context, men and women set themselves as judges of what the Lord has said. Instead of getting down on their knees and letting the Lord judge them, they stand with pride and judge the Lord.

I have the report of a youth meeting held in a large and well-known church in Toronto. The guest speaker was brought to the city so he could give this kind of counsel to modern church young people: "Don't believe anything in the Bible that does not square with your own experience!"

If you are among those who pick and choose, you may have chosen the beauties of nature as the means by which you bring yourself to worship. Or, you may be of the opinion that your worship comes through music, and you talk about music that elevates the mind and raises the soul to near rapture.

Now that we have mentioned nature and the inclination of some to let their worship begin and end there, I would like to put something in the record right here.

If you will really give yourself to study, you will discover that the Old Testament is a marvelous rhapsody on the natural creation. Start with Moses, and when you get beyond the Levitical order, you will find him soaring in his acute consciousness of the presence of God in all of creation.

Go on to the book of Job, and in the closing sections you will be amazed at the sublimity of the language describing the world around us.

Then go on to the Psalms, and you will find David literally dancing with ecstatic delight as he gazes out upon the wonders of God's world.

Begin reading in Isaiah and you will find the loftiest imagery. It is neither fanciful nor flighty but a presentation of the wonders of creation as the prophet observed them.

These men, who were some of the holiest and godliest men of that ancient time, revealed in their writings that they were intensely in love with every natural beauty around them. But always they saw nature as the handiwork of an all-powerful, all-wise, glorious Creator.

Now, allow me one further observation here about our civilization and our society.

I consider it a sad and lamentable fact that men and women generally today are like zoo lions born in captivity. They are born in hospitals, walk on concrete sidewalks, breathe a lot of foul air and are finally taken back to the hospital to die. They never really get a chance to get their feet into the soil.

How rarely do we get into a situation where we can feel the impulses of nature communicated to our beings. We seldom lift our eyes to look at God's heaven above except when an airplane crosses overhead or we are wondering whether we should wear our boots. In the very midst of the myriad of created wonders all around us, we have almost unknowingly lost the capacity to wonder.

If the Holy Spirit should come again upon us as in earlier times, visiting church congregations with the sweet but fiery breath of Pentecost, we would be greater Christians and holier souls. Beyond that, we would also be greater poets and greater artists and greater lovers of God and of His universe.

Men and women continue to try to persuade themselves that there are many forms and ways that seem right in worship. But God in His revelation has told us that He is spirit and those who worship Him must worship Him in spirit and in truth. God takes the matter of worship out of the hands of men and puts it in the hands of the Holy Spirit.

It is impossible for any of us to worship God without

the impartation of the Holy Spirit. It is the operation of the Spirit of God within us that enables us to worship God acceptably through that person we call Jesus Christ, who is Himself God.

So worship originates with God and comes back to us and is reflected from us, as a mirror. God accepts no other kind of worship.

We live in a mixed-up kind of world in which many, many people are not at all sure of what they believe or what they ought to believe. Most of them excuse it by telling us that they are "seekers after truth."

Some churches advertise that way—you do not have to believe anything; "just be a seeker after truth."

People who do not acknowledge the new birth or the leadings of the Holy Spirit acknowledge the ancient impulse to "worship something." If they are not educated, they might kill a chicken and put feathers on their heads and dance around in a little circle. We call them witch doctors. If they are educated, they might write poetry instead, and it comes out something like Edwin Markham's "I Made a Pilgrimage to Find the Gods."

Many persons are prepared to say with Markham that they "saw his bright hand sending signals from the sun." I, for one, never had any such signals. We live in a land where Bibles are everywhere, and the gospel is being preached faithfully. Yet men and women seek God in old altars and tombs in dark and dusty places. They finally wind up believing that God is sending signals from the sun.

Someone generally gets mad at me when I say that this kind of seeking after "truth" needs to be exposed. We need to double our efforts to tell the world that God is Spirit, and those who worship Him must worship Him in spirit and in truth (see John 4:23).

It must be by the Holy Spirit and truth. We cannot worship in the spirit alone, for the spirit without truth is helpless. We cannot worship in truth alone, for that would be theology without fire.

Worship must be in spirit and in truth!

It must be the truth of God and the Spirit of God. When a person, yielding to God and believing the truth of God, is filled with the Spirit of God, even his faintest whisper will be worship.

The stark, tragic fact is that the efforts of many people to worship are unacceptable to God. Without an infusion of the Holy Spirit, there can be no true worship. This is serious. It is hard for me to rest peacefully at night knowing that millions of cultured, religious people are merely carrying on church traditions and religious customs and they are not actually reaching God at all.

We must humbly worship God in spirit and in truth. Each one of us stands before the truth to be judged. Is it not now plain that the presence and the power of the Holy Spirit of God, far from being an optional luxury in our Christian lives, is a necessity?

CHAPTER 4

BORN TO WORSHIP GOD

And unto Adam he said, Because thou hast hearkened unto the voice of thy wife, and hast eaten of the tree, of which I commanded thee, saying, Thou shalt not eat of it: cursed is the ground for thy sake; in sorrow shalt thou eat of it all the days of thy life;

Thorns also and thistles shall it bring forth to thee; and thou shalt eat the herb of the field;

In the sweat of thy face shalt thou eat bread, till thou return unto the ground; for out of it wast thou taken: for dust thou art, and unto dust shalt thou return.

And Adam called his wife's name Eve; because she was the mother of all living.

Unto Adam also and to his wife did the LORD God make coats of skins, and clothed them.

And the LORD God said, Behold, the man is become as one of us, to know good and evil: and now, lest he put forth his hand, and take also of the tree of life, and eat, and live for ever:

Therefore the LORD God sent him forth from the garden of Eden, to till the ground from whence he was taken.

So he drove out the man; and he placed at the east of the garden of Eden Cherubims, and a flaming sword which

turned every way, to keep the way of the tree of life.
(Genesis 3:17–24)

One of the greatest tragedies that we find, even in this most enlightened of all ages, is the utter failure of millions of men and women ever to discover why they were born.

Deny it if you will—and some persons will—but wherever there are humans in this world, there are people who are suffering from a hopeless and depressing kind of amnesia. It forces them to cry out, either silently within themselves or often with audible frustration, "I don't even know why I was born!"

For an illustration, I want to share a story with you, a story that could have happened anywhere. It concerns a man who lost his memory and thus lost his identity.

Having to meet a friend at City Hall, I was waiting, seated on a bench near the walkway. Suddenly, a nicely dressed young man came over and took the seat beside me.

He smiled at me—a rather puzzled smile, I thought.

"Do we know each other?" I asked.

"No, I don't think so," he replied. Then he added, "I think I am in some kind of a jam."

He went on, "Something has happened to me. I think I tripped and fell somewhere in the city and bumped my head. I cannot remember anything for sure. When I woke up I had been robbed. My wallet and all of my cards and papers were gone. I have no identification—and I do not know who I am."

"You must have a family somewhere; don't you have any recollection?"

"I probably have, but I cannot recall."

I was about to tell this puzzled fellow that he would have to go to the police because I did not have any means of helping him. Just then I noticed a distinguished gentleman standing on the sidewalk near us. He too looked rather puzzled and uncertain, but as he glanced toward our bench, he let out a sudden, delighted shout—almost a scream.

He rushed over to us and called my bewildered friend by his name. He grabbed him quickly and shook his hand. "Where have you been, and what have you been doing? Everyone in the orchestra is worried sick about you."

The lost man was still bewildered.

"Pardon me, sir, but I do not know you. I do not recognize you."

"What? You do not know me? We came to Toronto together three days ago. Don't you know that we are members of the Philharmonic and that you are the first violinist? We have filled our engagement without you, and we have been searching everywhere for you!"

"So that is who I am, and that is why I am here! But I still don't know whether I can play a violin."

Incidents similar to this are taking place among persons all over the world. The police continue to look for many amnesia victims, and doctors are facing this problem with many patients.

Now, why have I told this story? To remind you of our first parents in the human race: the man named Adam and the woman named Eve.

Adam had a fall, and he received a terrible bump; involved with him in the catastrophe was Eve, his wife. Then, when they tried to shake the fog out of their minds, looking at each other, they realized that they no longer knew who they were, and they did not know why they were alive. They did not know the purpose for their existence.

Ever since that time, men and women alienated from God and trying to exist on a sick, fallen planet have been pleading, "I don't even know why I was born!"

Those who have followed the revelation provided by the Creator God have accepted that God never does anything without a purpose. We do believe, therefore, that God had a noble purpose in mind when He created us. We believe that it was distinctly the will of God that men and women created in His image would desire fellowship with Him above all else.

In His plan, it was to be a perfect fellowship based on adoring worship of the Creator and Sustainer of all things.

If you are acquainted with the Shorter Catechism, you know that it asks an age-old, searching question: "What is the chief end of man?"

The simple yet profound answer provided by the catechism is based upon the revelation and wisdom of the Word of God: "The chief end of man is to glorify God and to enjoy Him forever." That needs no translation for a thinking person. To worship and glorify God—that is the chief end of any man or woman.

Why have so many people missed it? Why have so many remained ignorant of God's love and God's plan throughout an entire lifetime? Why do so many curse all of the unkind situations in their lives, finally crying out in hopeless despair, "Oh, I don't even know why I was ever born into this world!"?

How could the Creator's desired will for all the sons and daughters of Adam be so thoroughly frustrated, so completely ruled out?

In this day of rampant sin, violence and transgression, we must point out that there is an almost universal denial of the willful and sinful fall of the human race, faithfully recorded in the book of Genesis.

Let me assure you that it is only through the revelation of God in His Word that we are able to learn the things we need to know about ourselves.

God's Word tells us frankly of the great injury we suffered, resulting in our numbing amnesia. It is the sad record of man's fall from the perfections of his original state. When Adam and Eve decided in that early morning that they had a right to put their own wills above the will of their Creator God, they experienced a terrible fall. The result: They lost their God-given identity.

They tried to shake the fog out of their minds and out of their beings, but as they looked at each other, they realized that they no longer knew the purpose of their existence.

They had suddenly been afflicted with a strange amnesia, precipitated by their willful sin of disobedience. They no longer knew precisely where they were. They no longer held that divine sense of what they were created to be and to do.

What a tragedy! Created to be a mirror to the Almighty, Adam and Eve forfeited the glory of God. Made in God's image, Adam and Eve were more like Him than the angels above.

God had created man so He could look into him and see reflected there more of His own glory than He could see reflected in the starry skies above.

But now the mirror was dimmed and blurred. When God would look at sinful man, He no longer could see His own glory.

Disobedient man had become sinful man. He had failed to fulfill the purpose of his creation—to worship his Creator in the beauty of holiness.

Men and women in our time, tired and guilty and lost, are too engaged with the tragedies of their own families and their own societies to look back at the great, overwhelming tragedy that we call the Fall of man.

It is a compounded tragedy because God had said with pleasure, "Let us make man in our image" (Genesis 1:26). Then stooping down, God took up clay, shaped and formed man and blew the breath of life into his nostrils. God's man had become a living soul.

The Creator then asked the man to look around at the rest of the creation.

"This is all yours—and I am yours," God said. "I will look at you and see in your face the reflection of My own glory. That is your end. You are created to worship Me, to glorify Me and to have Me as your God forever."

But when God withdrew for a moment, that evil one, the dragon who is called Satan, poisoned the minds of the man and his bride. They sinned against God.

When God returned, He came as though He did not know about the tragedy. He called out, "Adam, where are you?" Adam came out of hiding, knowing full well his guilt and his shame.

God said, "Adam, what did you do?"

Adam confessed, "We ate from the fruit of the tree that you forbade us to eat—but it was the woman who enticed me!"

God said to the woman, "What did you do?" and she said, "It was the serpent that beguiled me!"

In that brief time our first parents had learned the art of laying the blame on someone else. That is one of the great, betraying evidences of sin—and we have learned it straight from our first parents. We do not accept the guilt of our sin and iniquity. We blame someone else.

If you are not the man you ought to be, you are likely to blame your wife, or your ancestors, or perhaps the place where you work. If you are not the young person you ought to be, you can always blame your parents. If you are not the wife or woman you ought to be, you may blame your husband, or perhaps the children.

Sin being what it is, we would rather lay the blame on others. We blame, blame, blame. That is why we are where we are.

That is why disease fastens on us and drags us to death. That is why accidents come. That is why there are jails and mental hospitals and graveyards. Yes, all because of the great tragedy and disaster that we call the Fall of man.

Is this the final end? Is this all there is?

No, no! This is our answer to everyone in the entire human race: We have wonderful news for you! It is the good news that the God who created us did not give us up. He did not say to the angels, "Write them off and blot them from My memory."

Rather, He said, "Oh, I still want them! I still want them to be a mirror in which I can look and see My glory. I still want to be admired by My people. I still want My people to enjoy Me and have Me forever."

So God sent His only begotten Son through the miracle of the Incarnation. When Jesus walked the earth, He was the reflected glory of God. The New Testament says that He is the effulgence of God's glory and the brightness of His person (see Hebrews 1:3). When God looked at Mary's son, He saw Himself reflected.

What did Jesus mean when He told the people of His day, "When you have seen Me you have seen the Father"?

(see John 14:9).

He was actually saying, "When you see Me, you are seeing the Father's glory reflected. I have come to finish the work He has given Me to do."

God was glorified in His Son, even though at His Son's death the glory was terribly marred. Sinful men plucked His beard, bruised His face, tore out His hair. They made great blue lumps on His forehead. Then they nailed Him to the cross. There He groaned and sweated and suffered for six hours before He finally gave up His spirit and died.

The bells in heaven rang out because lost man had now been redeemed. The way of pardon and forgiveness had been opened for sinners.

On the third day, Jesus arose from the dead. Since then He has been at God's right hand. God has been busy redeeming people back to Himself, back to the original purpose of their being mirrors of His glory.

Yes, worship of the loving God is man's whole reason for existence. That is why we are born, and that is why we are born again from above. That is why we were created, and that is why we have been recreated. That is why there was a genesis at the beginning, and that is why there is a re-genesis, called regeneration.

That is also why there is a church. The Christian church exists to worship God first of all. Everything else must come second or third or fourth or fifth.

In Europe many generations ago, the dear old saint of God Brother Lawrence was on his deathbed. Rapidly losing his physical strength, he witnessed to those gathered around him: "I am not dying. I am just doing what I have been doing for the past forty years, and doing what I expect to be doing for all eternity!"

"What is that?" he was asked. He replied quickly, "I

am worshipping the God I love!"

Worshipping God—that was primary for Brother Lawrence. He was also dying, but that was secondary. He knew why he had been born into this world—and he knew why he had been born again.

Yes, and Brother Lawrence is still worshipping God. He died and they buried his body somewhere, but his was a living soul, created in the image of God. So, he is still worshipping with all the saints around the throne of God.

Sad, sad indeed, are the cries of so many today who have never discovered why they were born. It brings to mind the poet Milton's description of the pathetic lost-ness and loneliness of our first parents. Driven from the garden, he says, "They took hand in hand and through the valley made their solitary way."

CHAPTER 5

WE MUST WORSHIP ONLY THE ETERNAL GOD

Know ye not that ye are the temple of God, and that the Spirit of God dwelleth in you?

If any man defile the temple of God, him shall God destroy; for the temple of God is holy, which temple ye are.

Let no man deceive himself. If any man among you seemeth to be wise in this world, let him become a fool, that he may be wise.

For the wisdom of this world is foolishness with God. For it is written, He taketh the wise in their own craftiness.

And again, The Lord knoweth the thoughts of the wise, that they are vain.

Therefore let no man glory in men. For all things are yours;

Whether Paul, or Apollos, or Cephas, or the world, or life, or death, or things present, or things to come; all are yours;

And ye are Christ's; and Christ is God's. (1 Corinthians 3:16–23)

Technology is paramount in this generation. Much of our thinking about worship reflects a willingness to exchange a high view of God's eternity for a short-term concept called here and now.

My ministries in the Word of God have not been marked by any running controversy with true science. I have voiced my suspicions about a variety of views that can be traced to pseudoscience—views that generally try to throw God out the window of His universe. I could never worship a God who was not concerned with our eternities.

On the other hand, the answers science gives us are short-term answers. The scientist might be able to keep us alive for a few extra years but believing Christians know some things that Einstein did not know.

For instance, we know why we are here. We can say why we were born. We also know what we believe about the value of things eternal.

I confess that I used to try to read the theories about such things as the fourth dimension. But years ago I gave up trying to understand them.

I have nothing against science and its claim to seek after the meaning of things and their relation and inter-action. I am not about to ignorantly refute the scientist.

This is my position: Let the scientist stay in his field, and I will stay in mine. I am as glad and thankful as any-one for the benefits of research, and I hope scientists will soon find the cure for heart disease, for I have lost many good friends from sudden heart attacks.

But listen to me now about the difference in meaning between the short-term matters of our physical beings and the eternal relationship between the believer and his God.

If you save a person from diptheria when he is a baby, or save him in his teens from smallpox, or save him in his fifties from a heart attack, what have you done?

If that man lives to be ninety and still is without God and does not know why he was born, you have simply perpetuated the life of a mud turtle. That man who has never found God and has never been born again is like a turtle, with two legs instead of four and no shell and no tail, because he still does not know what life has been all about.

I am thankful that I have found a promise from the God of all grace that deals with the long term and the eternal. I belong to a company of plain people who believes the truth revealed in the Bible. These are the people who believe that God in the beginning made the heavens and the earth and all things that are therein. We believe that it was God who made man in His own image and breathed into him the breath of life and said unto him, "Now, live in My presence and worship Me—for that is your chief end. Increase and multiply and fill the earth with worshippers."

Yes, these plain people, these believing people, will tell you that God created the flowers to be beautiful and the birds to sing so that men and women could enjoy them. The scientist, with an entirely different kind of perspective, would never admit that fact. The scientist contends that the bird sings for a totally different reason.

"It is the male bird that sings, and he sings only to attract the female so they may nest and procreate," he tells us. "It is simply biological."

It is at this point that I ask the scientist, "Why doesn't the bird just squeak or groan or gurgle? Why does he have to sing and warble and harmonize as though he had been tuned to a harp?"

I think the answer is plain—it is because God made him to sing.

If I were a male bird and wanted to attract a female, I could turn handsprings or do any number of tricks. But why does the bird sing so beautifully?

It is because the God who made him is the Chief Musician of the universe. He is the Composer of the cosmos. He made the harp in those little throats and the feathers around them and said, "Go and sing."

Thankfully, the birds obeyed and they have been singing and praising God ever since they were created.

The scientific man may protest and say, "No, no!" But my heart tells me that it is so, and the Bible declares that it is so. "He hath made every thing beautiful in his time" (Ecclesiastes 3:11).

Again, God made the fruit trees to bear fruit for the human race. But the scientist shrugs his shoulders and says, "Of course the trees bear fruit so there will be seeds and thus there will be reproduction of more fruit." We have the right to reply, "Why is it so necessary for the tree to bear fruit if reproduction is all that is involved, with no blessing or help for anyone?"

God made the fruit and said to mankind, "Enjoy it."

God also made the beasts of the field in order that mankind could be clothed. God made the sheep with his coat of wool so he could be sheared and provide the sweaters and garments that keep us warm.

God made the humble little silkworm, providing the mulberry leaves for its food, so the silkworm could spin its cocoon. Men have discovered how to unravel the cocoons and produce the lovely silks that we admire so much.

I am not exactly one of the world's ten best-dressed men, but I like a nice silk tie better than any of those synthetic ones rolled out of a manufacturer's vat somewhere.

Oh, it is so much more delightful and satisfying to believe what God says about all of these things He has given us to enjoy—everything having its purpose.

Actually, the wisest person in the world is the person who knows the most about God. The only real sage worthy of the name is the one who realizes that the answer to creation and life and eternity is a theological answer—not a scientific answer.

You must begin with God. Then you begin to understand everything in its proper context. All things fit into shape and form when you begin with God.

I wonder if you will understand me when I say what I am going to say. Quite a few evangelical Christians have been acquiring a rather bad habit—the habit of being unduly influenced by the degrees and the honors bestowed upon those whom we consider "the learned."

This undue deference to intellectual knowledge and accomplishment has to be balanced out. As Christian men and women, we do respect study and research. We appreciate the long hours that go into academic progress. But we must always keep God's wisdom and God's admonitions in mind.

No matter how much education and training we might receive in a certain field of study, we will discover that we have only learned scattered fragments of truth. On the other hand, the simplest Christian believer, who might have come into the kingdom only a few days ago, has already learned many marvelous things at the center of truth. That believer is able to confess that he knows God. Knowing God is potentially more than all of this world's teachers could ever impart, because those teachers, if they are without God, are on the outside looking in.

There is a miracle involved here. That new believer, who only a few days ago was a sinner lost and unforgiven, is now by faith and through grace a child of God and on the inside looking out!

We do not belittle the many accomplishments of those who are learned and able in this world's store of knowledge. But to study and toil for this world alone is not enough. The key is God. He rightfully belongs in the middle of all our endeavors. All of the doors must ultimately be opened, through faith, with the key called God.

If we are to have any satisfying and lasting understanding of life, it must be divinely given. It begins with the confession that it is indeed the God who has revealed Himself to us who is the great central pillar bearing up the universe.

Believing that, we then go on to acknowledge that we have thus discovered His great eternal purpose. God made us as men and women in His own image. He has now redeemed and restored us through His plan of salvation to love Him and worship Him forever.

God said, "I have made man in My image and man is to be above all other creatures. He is to be above the beasts of the earth and the birds of the air and the fish in the sea (see Genesis 1:26). Redeemed man is to be even above the angels in the heavens. He is to enter into My presence pardoned and unashamed. He is to worship Me and to look on My face while the ages roll on."

God is the only certain foundation. The joy of assurance belongs to believing people. I associated myself with them when I was converted at the age of seventeen. Until that time I knew nothing of love or hope or trust or faith in God. There are millions today who are just as lost as I was. They are still without God, confused about this life and lacking knowledge of the life to come.

The believing Christians about whom I am talking are the saints and the mystics, the people of God. They have a simple and more beautiful view of the world than the scientists hold. It is simply this: "We know what we believe. We know we are in this world to worship and to enjoy God. We know what God is prepared to do for all those who love Him, throughout eternity."

Thus, they know some important long-range things. These things are hidden from other men and women who are trying to find their answers in the store of knowledge related to this present world.

The average person in the world today, without faith and without God and without hope, is engaged in a desperate personal search throughout his lifetime. He does not really know where he has been. He does not really know what he is doing here and now. He does not know where he is going.

The sad commentary is that he is doing it all on borrowed time and borrowed money and borrowed strength—and he already knows that in the end he will surely die! It boils down to the bewildered confession of many that "we have lost God somewhere along the way."

What happens to people when they lose God? It seems quite obvious that they get very busy trying to find something else to worship.

Man, made more like God than any other creature, has become less like God than any other creature. Created to reflect the glory of God, he has retreated sullenly into his cave—reflecting only his own sinfulness.

Certainly it is a tragedy above all tragedies in this world that man, made with a soul to worship and praise and sing to God's glory, now sulks silently in his cave. Love has gone from his heart. Light has gone from his mind. Having lost God, he blindly stumbles on through this dark world to find only a grave at the end.

In a radio interview a brilliant, well-known Canadian author was being questioned about the modern world scene. He was asked a searching question: "What do you consider the most alarming error we are making in our current society and civilization?"

His answer was quick and to the point: "I consider our biggest mistake to be the fond belief that we humans are special pets of Almighty God; that we mean more than other things in the world; that God has a special fondness for us as people."

Oh, brother!

Man as he was originally created is God's beloved. Man is the beloved of the universe.

Since I learned that Christ Jesus came into the world to be my Savior (see 1 Timothy 1:15), I have based my life on God's revelation in the Scriptures. No matter how brilliant a man's mind might be, he cannot jar me as far as the things of God are concerned. He throws his objections and his earthly conclusions at me with no effect.

Actually, the differences between unbelief and faith, between hopelessness and certainty, between man's point of view and God's, often come to light as the believer faces death.

We are told that when John Wesley was dying, he tried to sing, but his voice was nearly gone. He was almost ninety. He had traveled hundreds of thousands of miles on horseback, preaching three or four times daily in founding a great church. He was plainly Arminian in his theology, but as his Christian family and friends gathered around his bed, he was trying to sing the words of an old Calvinist hymn:

> I will praise my Maker while I've breath,
> And when my soul is lost in death,
> Praise shall employ my nobler powers.

That is why I cannot get all heated up about contending for one theological side or another on that issue. If Isaac Watts, a Calvinist, could write such praise to God and John Wesley, an Arminian, could sing it with yearning and they both can meet and hug one another in glory, why should I allow anyone to force me to confess, "I don't know which I am!" Why should anyone bother me with an issue like that?

I was created to worship and praise God. I was redeemed that I should worship Him and enjoy Him forever.

That is the primary issue, my brother or sister. That is why we earnestly invite men and women to become converted, taking Jesus Christ as their Savior and Lord.

God is not asking you to come to Christ just to attain peace of mind or to make you a better businessman or woman. You were created to worship. God wants you to know His redemption so you will desire to worship and praise Him.

Chapter 6

Awed by the Presence of God

In the year that king Uzziah died I saw also the Lord sitting upon a throne, high and lifted up, and his train filled the temple.

Above it stood the seraphims: each one had six wings; with twain he covered his face, and with twain he covered his feet, and with twain he did fly.

And one cried unto another, and said, Holy, holy, holy, is the Lord of hosts: the whole earth is full of his glory.

And the posts of the door moved at the voice of him that cried, and the house was filled with smoke.

Then said I, Woe is me! for I am undone; because I am a man of unclean lips, and I dwell in the midst of a people of unclean lips: for mine eyes have seen the King, the Lord of hosts.

Then flew one of the seraphims unto me, having a live coal in his hand, which he had taken with the tongs from off the altar:

And he laid it upon my mouth, and said, Lo, this hath touched thy lips; and thine iniquity is taken away, and thy sin purged.

Also I heard the voice of the Lord, saying, Whom shall I send, and who will go for us? Then said I, Here am I; send me. (Isaiah 6:1–8)

Through the years, I have quite often heard educated and intelligent persons say, "Let me tell you how I discovered God."

Whether these discoverers went on from there to a humble and adoring worship of God, I cannot say. I do know, however, that all of us would be in great trouble and still far from God if He had not graciously and in love revealed Himself to us.

I am a little irritated or grieved at the continuing hope of so many people that they will be able to grasp God—understand God, commune with God—through their intellectual capacities. When will they realize that if they could possibly "discover" God with the intellect, they would be equal to God?

We would do well to lean toward the kind of discovery of God described by the prophet Isaiah: In the year that king Uzziah died I saw also the Lord sitting upon a throne, high and lifted up, and his train filled the temple. (6:1)

Now, that which Isaiah saw was wholly other than, and altogether different from, anything he had ever seen before. Up to this point in his life, Isaiah had become familiar with the good things God had created. But he had never been introduced to the presence of the Uncreated.

To Isaiah, then, the violent contrast between that which is God and that which is not God was such that his very language suffered under the effort to express it.

Significantly, God was revealing Himself to man. Isaiah could have tried for a million years to reach God by means of his intellect without any chance of succeeding.

All of the accumulated brainpower in the whole world could not reach God.

But the living God, in the space of a short second of time, can reveal Himself to the willing spirit of a man. It is only then that an Isaiah, or any other man or woman, can say with humility but with assurance, "I know Him."

Unlike men, God never acts without purpose. Here God was revealing Himself to Isaiah for eternal purposes. Isaiah has tried to give us a true record, but what actually happened is greater than what Isaiah wrote by as much as God is greater than the human mind. Isaiah confesses that he had never before seen the Lord sitting upon a throne.

Modern critics of this record by Isaiah warn us of the danger of anthropomorphism—the attempt to bestow upon God certain human attributes.

I have never been afraid of big words. Let them call it what they will, I still believe that God sits upon a throne, invested with self-bestowed sovereignty. I believe, too, that God sits upon a throne determining all events, finally, according to the purpose that He purposed in Christ Jesus before the world began.

Now, because we are dealing with worship, let us consider the joys and delights of the heavenly creatures, the seraphim, around the throne of God. This is Isaiah's record:

> Above it stood the seraphims: each one had six wings; with twain he covered his face, and with twain he covered his feet, and with twain he did fly.

> And one cried unto another, and said, Holy, holy, holy, is the LORD of hosts: the whole earth is full of his glory. (6:2–3)

We know very little about these created beings, but I

am impressed by their attitude of exalted worship. They are close to the throne, and they burn with rapturous love for the Godhead. They were engrossed in their antiphonal chants, "Holy, holy, holy!"

I have often wondered why the rabbis and saints and hymnists of those olden times did not come to the knowledge of the Trinity just from the seraphims' praise, "Holy, holy, holy." I am a Trinitarian—I believe in one God, the Father Almighty, maker of heaven and earth. I believe in one Lord Jesus Christ, Son of the Father, begotten of Him before all ages. I believe in the Holy Spirit, the Lord and giver of life, who with the Father and Son together is worshipped and glorified.

This is a very moving scene—the seraphim worshipping God. The more I read my Bible, the more I believe in the Triune God.

In Isaiah's vision the seraphim were chanting their praises to the Trinity eight hundred years before Mary cried with joy and her baby wailed in Bethlehem's manger, when the second person of the Trinity, the eternal Son, came to earth to dwell among us. The key words then and the keynote still of our worship must be, "Holy, holy, holy!"

I am finding that many Christians are really not comfortable with the holy attributes of God. In such cases I am forced to wonder about the quality of the worship they try to offer to Him.

The word *holy* is more than an adjective saying that God is a holy God—it is an ecstatic ascription of glory to the Triune God. I am not sure that we really know what it means, but I think we should attempt a definition.

Complete moral purity can only describe God. Everything that appears to be good among men and women must be discounted, for we are human. Not one of us is morally pure. Abraham, David and Elijah; Moses, Peter and Paul—all were good men. They were included in God's fellowship. But each had his human flaws and weaknesses as members of Adam's race. Each had to find the place of humble repentance. Because God knows our hearts and our intentions, He is able to restore His sincere and believing children who are in the faith.

Much of our problem in continuing fellowship with a holy God is that many Christians repent only for what they do, rather than for what they are.

It should help us to be concerned about the quality of our worship when we consider that Isaiah's reaction was a feeling of absolute profaneness in the presence of the moral purity of the divine being. Consider that Isaiah was a commendable young man—cultured, religious and a cousin of the king. He would have made a good deacon in any church. Today he would be asked to serve on one of our mission boards.

But here Isaiah was an astonished man. He was struck with awe, his whole world suddenly dissolving into a vast, eternal brightness. He was pinned against that brightness—red and black, the colors of sin.

What had happened? Isaiah, only human, had glimpsed One whose character and nature signaled perfection. He could only manage the witness: "Mine eyes have seen the King."

The definition of "Holy, holy" must certainly have room for "mystery" if, in our attempts to worship, we are to have an effective appreciation of our God.

There are leaders in various Christian circles who know so much about the things of God that they will offer to answer every question you might have.

We can hope to answer questions helpfully as far as we can. But there is a sense of divine mystery running throughout all of the kingdom of God—far beyond the mystery that scientists discover running throughout the kingdom of nature.

There are those who pretend to know everything about God—who pretend they can explain everything about God, about His creation, about His thoughts and about His judgments. They have joined the ranks of the evangelical rationalists. They end up taking the mystery out of life and the mystery out of worship. When they have done that, they have taken God out as well.

The kind of "know-it-all" attitude about God that we see in some teachers today leaves them in a very difficult position. They must roundly criticize and condemn any other man taking any position slightly different from theirs.

Our cleverness and glibness and fluency may well betray our lack of that divine awe upon our spirits, silent and wonderful, that breathes a whisper, "Oh, Lord God, Thou knowest."

In Isaiah 6 we see a clear portrayal of what happens to a person in the mystery of the Presence. Isaiah, overpowered within his own being, can only confess humbly, "I am a man of unclean lips!"

I remind you that Isaiah recognized the "strangeness"—something of the mystery of the person of God. In that Presence, Isaiah found no place for joking or for clever cynicism or for human familiarity. He found a strangeness in God—that is, a presence unknown to the sinful and worldly and self-sufficient human.

A person who has sensed what Isaiah sensed will never be able to joke about "the Man upstairs" or the "Someone up there who likes me."

One of the movie actresses who still prowled around the nightclubs after her supposed conversion to Christ was quoted as telling someone, "You ought to know God. You know, God is just a livin' doll!" I read where another man said, "God is a good fellow."

I confess that when I hear or read these things, I feel a great pain within. My brother or sister, there is something about our God that is different, that is beyond us, that is above us—transcendent. We must be humbly willing to throw our hearts open and to plead, "God, shine Thyself into my understanding for I will never find Thee otherwise."

The mystery, the strangeness is in God. Our Lord does not expect us to behave like zombies when we become Christians. But He does expect that we will have our soul open to the mystery that is God. I think it is proper for us to say that a genuine Christian should be a walking mystery because he surely is a walking miracle. Through the leading and the power of the Holy Spirit, the Christian is involved in a daily life and habit that cannot be explained. A Christian should have upon him an element that is beyond psychology—beyond all natural laws and into spiritual laws.

"God is a consuming fire" (Deuteronomy 4:24). We are told that "it is a fearful thing to fall into the hands of the living God" (Hebrews 10:31). Do you recall the first chapter of Ezekiel? The dejected prophet saw heaven opened. He was given a vision of God. And he then witnessed four-faced creatures out of the fire.

I think in our witness and ministries, we Christians should be men and women out of the fire. Because our God is holy, He is actively hostile to sin. God can only burn on and on against sin forever. In another passage Isaiah asked, "Who among us shall dwell with the devouring fire? who among us shall dwell with everlasting burnings?" (33:14).

Isaiah was not thinking about those who would be separated from God. He was thinking of a company who would live for God and dwell with God. He answers his own question: "He that walketh righteously, and speaketh uprightly; . . . he shall dwell on high" (33:15–16).

The Salvation Army has always had as its slogan "Blood and Fire." I am for that in the things of God. We know of cleansing by the blood of Christ. The references to God's workings often have to do with a holy flame. John the Baptist pointed to Christ's coming and said, "I indeed baptize you with water unto repentance. . . . he shall baptize you with the Holy Ghost, and with fire" (Matthew 3:11).

When Isaiah cried out, "I am undone!" it was a cry of pain. It was the revealing cry of conscious uncleanness. He was experiencing the undoneness of the creature set over against the holiness of the Creator.

What should happen in genuine conversion? What should a man or woman feel in the transaction of the new birth?

There ought to be that real and genuine cry of pain. That is why I do not like the kind of evangelism that tries to invite people into the fellowship of God by signing a card.

There should be a birth from above and within. There should be the terror of seeing ourselves in violent contrast to the holy, holy, holy God. Unless we come into this place of conviction and pain, I am not sure how deep and real our repentance will ever be.

Today, it is not a question of whether we have Isaiah's cleanness, but a question of whether we have his awareness. He was unclean and, thank God, he became aware of it. But the world today is unclean and seems to be almost totally unaware of it. Uncleanness with unawareness will have terrible consequences. That is what is wrong with the Christian church and with our Protestantism. Our problem is the depravity still found within the circle of the just, among those called to be saints, among those who claim to be great souls.

We like Isaiah's vision and awareness. But we do not like to think of the live coal out of the fire being placed on the prophet's lips.

Purification by blood and by fire. Isaiah's lips, symbolic of all his nature, were purified by fire. God could then say to him, "Thine iniquity is taken away" (Isaiah 6:7).

That is how the amazed and pained Isaiah could genuinely come to a sense of restored moral innocence. That is how he instantly found that he was ready for worship and that he was also ready and anxious for service in the will of God.

With each of us, if we are to have that assurance of forgiveness and restored moral innocence, the fire of God's grace must touch us. It is only through the depths of the forgiving love of God that men and women can be so restored and made ready to serve Him.

In the same vein, is there any other way in which we, the creatures of God, can become prepared and ready to worship Him?

I can only remind you of our great needs in this terrible day when men and women are trying their best to cut God down to their size. Many also believe that it is possible to gain control of the sovereign God and to think

Him down to a plane where they can use Him as they want to.

Even in our Christian circles we are prone to depend upon techniques and methods in the work that Christ has given us to do. Without a complete dependence upon the Holy Spirit, we can only fail. If we have been misled to believe that we can do Christ's work ourselves, it will never be done.

The man whom God will use must be undone. He must be a man who has seen the King in His beauty.

Let us never take anything for granted about ourselves, my brother or sister.

Do you know who gives me the most trouble? Do you know who I pray for the most in my pastoral work? Just myself. I do not say it to appear to be humble, for I have preached all my lifetime to people who are better than I.

I tell you again that God has saved us to be worshippers. May God show us a vision of ourselves that will disvalue us to the point of total devaluation. From there He can raise us up to worship Him and to praise Him and to witness.

Chapter 7

Genuine Worship
Involves Feeling

And Saul, yet breathing out threatenings and slaughter against the disciples of the Lord, went unto the high priest,

And desired of him letters to Damascus to the synagogues, that if he found any of this way, whether they were men or women, he might bring them bound unto Jerusalem.

And as he journeyed, he came near Damascus: and suddenly there shined round about him a light from heaven:

And he fell to the earth, and heard a voice saying unto him, Saul, Saul, why persecutest thou me?

And he said, Who art thou, Lord? And the Lord said, I am Jesus whom thou persecutest: it is hard for thee to kick against the pricks.

And he trembling and astonished said, Lord, what wilt thou have me to do? And the Lord said unto him, Arise, and go into the city, and it shall be told thee what thou must do.

And the men which journeyed with him stood speechless, hearing a voice, but seeing no man.

And Saul arose from the earth; and when his eyes were opened, he saw no man: but they led him by the hand,

and brought him into Damascus.

And he was three days without sight, and neither did eat nor drink. (Acts 9:1–9)

How long do you think it will be, if Jesus tarries, before some of the amazing new churches like those in the primitive Baliem Valley of Irian Jaya, Indonesia, will be sending gospel missionaries to Canada and the United States?

If that thought upsets you, you desperately need to read this chapter.

I have a reason for suggesting this as a possibility at some time in the future. In Chicago, I was introduced to a deeply serious Christian brother who had come from his native India with a stirring and grateful testimony of the grace of God in his life.

I asked him about his church background, of course. He was not Pentecostal. He was neither Anglican nor Baptist. He was neither Presbyterian nor Methodist.

He did not even know what we mean by the label, "interdenominational." He was simply a brother in Christ.

This Indian had been born into the Hindu religion, but he was converted to and became a disciple of Jesus Christ by reading and seriously studying the New Testament record of the death and resurrection of our Lord.

He spoke English well enough to express his Christian concerns for the world and for the churches. I asked him to speak in my pulpit.

Through that encounter I realized that unless we arouse ourselves spiritually, unless we are brought back to genuine love and adoration and worship, our candlestick could be removed. We might need missionaries coming to us, indeed. We might need them to show us what genuine and vital Christianity is!

We should never forget that God created us to be joyful worshippers, but sin drew us into everything else but worship. Then in God's love and mercy in Christ Jesus, we were restored into the fellowship of the Godhead through the miracle of the new birth.

"You have been forgiven and restored," God reminds us. "I am your Creator and Redeemer and Lord, and I delight in your worship."

I don't know, my friend, how that makes you feel—but I feel that I must give God the full response of my heart. I am happy to be counted as a worshipper.

Well, that word "feel" has crept in here, and I know that you might have an instant reaction against it. In fact, I have had people tell me very dogmatically that they will never allow "feeling" to have any part in their spiritual life and experience. I reply, "Too bad for you!" I say that because I have voiced a very real definition of what I believe true worship to be: Worship is to feel in the heart!

In the Christian faith, we should be able to use the word "feel" boldly and without apology. What worse thing could be said of us as the Christian church if it could be said that we are a feelingless people?

Worship must always come from an inward attitude. It embodies a number of factors, including the mental, spiritual and emotional. You might not at times worship with the same degree of wonder and love that you do at other times, but the attitude and the state of mind are consistent if you are worshipping the Lord.

A husband and father might not appear to love and cherish his family with the same intensity when he is discouraged, when he is tired from long hours in business or when events have made him feel depressed.

He might not outwardly show as much love toward his

family, but it is there, nonetheless, for it is not a feeling only. It is an attitude and a state of mind. It is a sustained act, subject to varying degrees of intensity and perfection.

I came into the kingdom of God with joy, knowing that I had been forgiven. I do know something of the emotional life that goes along with conversion to Christ.

I well remember, however, that in my early Christian fellowship, there were those who warned me about the dangers of "feeling." They cited the biblical example of Isaac feeling the arms of Jacob and thinking they were Esau's. Thus the man who went by his feelings was mistaken!

That sounds interesting, but it is not something on which you can build Christian doctrine.

Think of that sick woman in the gospel record who had had an issue of blood for twelve years and had suffered many things of many physicians.

Mark records that when she had heard of Jesus, she came in the throng and merely touched His garment. In the same instant "the fountain of her blood was dried up; and she felt in her body that she was healed of that plague" (Mark 5:29).

Knowing what had been done within her by the Savior, she "came and fell down before him, and told him all the truth" (5:33). Her testimony was in worship and praise. She felt in her body that she was healed.

Those of us who have been blessed within our own beings would not join in any crusade to "follow your feelings." On the other hand, if there is no feeling at all in our hearts, then we are dead!

If you wake up tomorrow morning and there is absolute numbness in your right arm—no feeling at all—you will quickly dial the doctor with your good left hand.

Real worship is, among other things, a feeling about the Lord our God. It is in our hearts. And we must be willing to express it in an appropriate manner.

We can express our worship to God in many ways. But if we love the Lord and are led by His Holy Spirit, our worship will always bring a delighted sense of admiring awe and a sincere humility on our part.

The proud and lofty man or woman cannot worship God any more acceptably than can the proud devil himself. There must be humility in the heart of the person who would worship God in spirit and in truth.

The manner in which many moderns think about worship makes me uncomfortable. Can true worship be engineered and manipulated? Do you foresee with me the time to come when churches may call the pastor a "spiritual engineer"?

I have heard of psychiatrists being called "human engineers," and of course, they are concerned with our heads. We have reduced so many things to engineering or scientific or psychological terms that the coming of "spiritual engineers" is a possibility. But this will never replace what I have called the astonished wonder wherever worshippers are described in the Bible.

We find much of spiritual astonishment and wonder in the book of Acts. You will always find these elements present when the Holy Spirit directs believing men and women.

On the other hand, you will not find astonished wonder among men and women when the Holy Spirit is not present.

Engineers can do many great things in their fields, but no mere human force or direction can work the mysteries of God among men. If there is no wonder, no experience of mystery, our efforts to worship will be futile. There will be no worship without the Spirit.

If God can be understood and comprehended by any of our human means, then I cannot worship Him. One thing is sure: I will never bend my knees and say "Holy, holy, holy" to that which I have been able to decipher and figure out in my own mind! That which I can explain will never bring me to the place of awe. It can never fill me with astonishment or wonder or admiration.

The philosophers called the ancient mystery of the personhood of God the *mysterium conundrum*. We who are God's children by faith call Him "our Father which art in heaven." In sections of the church where there is life and blessing and wonder in worship, there is also the sense of divine mystery. Paul epitomized it for us as "Christ in you, the hope of glory" (Colossians 1:27).

What does happen, then, in a Christian church when a fresh and vital working of the Spirit of God brings revival? In my study and observations, a revival generally results in a sudden bestowment of a spirit of worship. This is not the result of engineering or of manipulation. It is something God bestows on people hungering and thirsting for Him. With spiritual renewing will come a blessed spirit of loving worship.

These believers worship gladly because they have a high view of God. In some circles, God has been abridged, reduced, modified, edited, changed and amended until He is no longer the God whom Isaiah saw, high and lifted up. Because He has been reduced in the minds of so many people, we no longer have that boundless confidence in His character that we used to have.

He is the God to whom we go without doubts, without fears. We know He will not deceive us or cheat us. He will not break His covenant or change His mind.

We have to be convinced so we can go into His presence in absolute confidence. In our hearts is this commitment: "Let God be true, but every man a liar" (Romans 3:4).

The God of the whole earth cannot do wrong! He does not need to be rescued. It is man's inadequate concept of God that needs to be rescued.

Thankfully, when God made us in His own image, He gave us the capability to appreciate and admire His attributes.

I once heard Dr. George D. Watson, one of the great Bible teachers of his generation, point out that men can have two kinds of love for God—the love of gratitude or the love of excellence. He urged that we go on from gratefulness to a love of God just because He is God and because of the excellence of His character.

Unfortunately, God's children rarely go beyond the boundaries of gratitude. I seldom hear anyone in worshipful prayer admiring and praising God for His eternal excellence.

Many of us are strictly "Santa Claus" Christians. We think of God as putting up the Christmas tree and putting our gifts underneath. That is only an elementary kind of love.

We need to go on. We need to know the blessing of worshipping in the presence of God without thought of wanting to rush out again. We need to be delighted in the presence of utter, infinite excellence.

Such worship will have the ingredient of fascination, of high moral excitement. Plainly, some of the men and women in the Bible knew this kind of fascination in their fellowship with God. If Jesus the Son is to be known and loved and served, the Holy Spirit must be allowed to illuminate our human lives. That personality will then be captured and entranced by the presence of God.

What is it that makes a human cry out:

O Jesus, Jesus, dearest Lord
Forgive me if I say,
For very love, Thy sacred name
A thousand times a day.

Burn, burn, O love, within my heart,
Burn fiercely night and day,
Till all the dross of earthly loves
Is burned, and burned away.

Those expressions came from the worshipping heart of Frederick W. Faber. He was completely fascinated by all he had experienced in the presence and fellowship of a loving God and Savior. He was surely filled with an intensity of moral excitement. He was struck with wonder at the inconceivable magnitude and moral splendor of the Being whom we call our God.

Such fascination with God must necessarily have an element of adoration. You may ask me for a definition of *adoration* in this context. I will say that when we adore God, all of the beautiful ingredients of worship are brought to white, incandescent heat with the fire of the Holy Spirit. To adore God means we love Him with all the powers within us. We love Him with fear and wonder and yearning and awe.

The admonition to "love the Lord thy God with all thy heart . . . and with all thy mind" (Matthew 22:37) can mean only one thing: to adore Him.

I use the word *adore* sparingly, for it is a precious word. I love babies and I love people, but I cannot say I adore them. Adoration I keep for the only One who deserves it. In no other presence and before no other being can I kneel in reverent fear and wonder and yearning and feel the sense of possessiveness that cries, "Mine, mine!"

They can change the expressions in the hymnals, but whenever men and women are lost in worship they will cry out, "O God, thou art my God; early will I seek thee" (Psalm 63:1). Worship becomes a completely personal love experience between God and the worshipper. It was like that with David, with Isaiah, with Paul. It is like that with all whose desire has been to possess God.

This is the glad truth: God is my God.

Brother or sister, until you can say God and I, you cannot say us with any meaning. Until you have been able to meet God in loneliness of soul, just you and God—as if there was no one else in the world—you will never know what it is to love the other persons in the world.

In Canada, those who have written of the saintly Holy Anne said, "She talks to God as if there was nobody else but God and He had no other children but her." That was not a selfish quality. She had found the value and delight of pouring her personal devotion and adoration at God's feet.

Consecration is not difficult for the person who has met God. Where there is genuine adoration and fascination, God's child wants nothing more than the opportunity to pour out his or her love at the Savior's feet.

A young man talked to me about his spiritual life. He had been a Christian for several years, but he was concerned that he might not be fulfilling the will of God for his life. He spoke of coldness of heart and lack of spiritual power. I could tell that he was discouraged—and afraid of hardness of heart.

I gave him a helpful expression that has come from

the writings of Bernard of Clairvaux: "My brother, only the heart is hard that does not know it is hard. Only he is hardened who does not know he is hardened. When we are concerned for our coldness, it is because of the yearning God has put there. God has not rejected us."

God puts the yearning and desire in our hearts, and He does not turn away and thus mock us. God asks us to seek His face in repentance and love, and we then find all of His gracious fullness awaiting. In God's grace, that is a promise for the whole wide world.

You have read of Blaise Pascal, the famous seventeenth century French scientist often classed as one of the six great thinkers of all time. He was considered a genius in mathematics, and his scientific inquiry was broad. He was a philosopher and a writer. But best of all, he experienced a personal, overwhelming encounter with God one night that changed his life.

Pascal wrote on a piece of paper a brief account of his experience, folded the paper and kept it in a pocket close to his heart, apparently as a reminder of what he had felt. Those who attended him at his death found the worn, creased paper. In Pascal's own hand it read:

> From about half-past ten at night to about half-after midnight—fire! O God of Abraham, God of Isaac, God of Jacob—not the God of the philosophers and the wise. The God of Jesus Christ who can be known only in the ways of the Gospel. Security—feeling—peace—joy— tears of joy. Amen.

Were these the expressions of a fanatic, an extremist?

No. Pascal's mind was one of the greatest. But the living God had broken through and beyond all that was human and intellectual and philosophical. The astonished Pascal could only describe in one word the visitation in his spirit: "Fire!"

Understand that this was not a statement in sentences for others to read. It was the ecstatic utterance of a yielded man during two awesome hours in the presence of his God.

There was no human engineering or manipulation there. There was only wonder and awe and adoration wrought by the presence of the Holy Spirit of God as Pascal worshipped.

What we need among us is a genuine visitation of the Spirit. We need a sudden bestowment of the spirit of worship among God's people.

CHAPTER 8

CHURCHES THAT FAIL GOD
FAIL ALSO IN WORSHIP

Till we all come in the unity of the faith, and of the knowledge of the Son of God, unto a perfect man, unto the measure of the stature of the fulness of Christ:

That we henceforth be no more children, tossed to and fro, and carried about with every wind of doctrine, by the sleight of men, and cunning craftiness, whereby they lie in wait to deceive;

But speaking the truth in love, may grow up into him in all things, which is the head, even Christ:

From whom the whole body fitly joined together and compacted by that which every joint supplieth, according to the effectual working in the measure of every part, maketh increase of the body unto the edifying of itself in love.

This I say therefore, and testify in the Lord, that ye henceforth walk not as other Gentiles walk, in the vanity of their mind,

Having the understanding darkened, being alienated from the life of God through the ignorance that is in them, because of the blindness of their heart.
(Ephesians 4:13–18)

Many people who feel they were "born into the church" and many who just take for granted their church traditions never stop to ask, "Why do we do what we do in the church and call it worship?"

It appears they have very little knowledge of, and probably even less appreciation for, the kind of Christian believers whom Peter describes as "a royal priesthood, an holy nation, a peculiar people" (1 Peter 2:9).

Let me ask, then, the question so many men and women with religious backgrounds never get around to asking. What is the real definition of the Christian church? What are the basic purposes for its existence?

Now, let me answer.

I believe a local church exists to do corporately what each Christian believer should be doing individually—and that is to worship God. It is to show forth the excellencies of Him who has called us out of darkness into his marvelous light (see 1 Peter 2:9). It is to reflect the glories of Christ ever shining upon us through the ministries of the Holy Spirit.

I am going to say something to you that will sound strange. It even sounds strange to me as I say it, because we are not used to hearing it within our Christian fellowships. We are saved to worship God. All that Christ has done for us in the past and all that He is doing now leads to this one end.

If we are denying this truth and if we are saying that worship is not really important, we can blame our attitudes for the great wave of arrested development in our Christian fellowships.

Why should the church of Jesus Christ be a spiritual school where hardly anyone ever graduates from the first grade?

You know the old joke about the man asked if he was well educated. "I should be," he answered. "I spent five years in the fourth grade."

There is no humor in the confession of any man or woman that he or she should be a good Christian, having spent the last nineteen years in the second and third grades of the Christian fellowship. When did anyone ever find in the Scriptures that the Christian church is dedicated to the proposition that everyone ought to remain static?

Whence came the notion that if you are a Christian and in the fold by faith you need never grow? On what authority are we not to worry about Christian maturity and spiritual development?

Ask people in church why they were converted, and you will get the answer: "So we could be happy, happy, happy! Everyone who is happy say 'Amen!'"

This condition is not isolated. It is the same all over North America and far beyond. I suppose all around the world we are seriously busy evangelizing and making more first graders.

It seems to be a bright and accepted idea that we can keep converts in the first grade until the Lord comes, and then He will give them rule over five cities.

Now, you who know me well know that I have not said these things about the church in an effort to be clever or to make fun of the church. Certainly I have not said them in any effort to appear "holier than thou."

We live in a time when the Spirit of God is saying to us, "How genuine are your concerns for lost men and women? How real are your prayers of concern for the church of Christ and its testimony to the world? How much agony of soul do you feel about the pressures of this life and modern society as they relate to the spiritual well-being of your own family?"

We will do great harm to the church and to those for whom we have love and concern if we do not recognize the kind of terrible day in which we live. Are you foolish enough to believe and expect that everything is going to remain just as it was, week after week, month after month, year after year?

Probably we are all better acquainted with Canadian and American and British history than with that of the rest of the world. But it is well to remember the history and the fate of Rome. One of the most civilized empires the world has known, Rome went down like a great rotten tree. She still had military strength and the show of power on the outside. But Rome had crumbled away on the inside. Rome doted on plenty of food and drink and on circuses and pleasure and, of course, on unbridled lust and immorality.

What great army put the Roman Empire down?

Rome fell before the barbarous hordes from the north—the Lombard, the Hun, the Ostrogoth—people who were not worthy even to care for the shoes of the Romans. Rome had become fat and weak and careless and unconcerned. And Rome died. The Roman Empire in the west ended when the last emperor, Romulus Augustulus, was deposed in AD 476.

The tragedy that happened to Rome on the inside is the same kind of threat that can harm and endanger a complacent and worldly church on the inside. It is hard for a proud, unconcerned church to function as a spiritual, mature and worshipping church. There is always the imminent danger of failure before God.

Many people loyal to the church and to forms and traditions deny that Christianity is showing any injury in our day. But it is the internal bleeding that brings death and decay. We might be defeated in the hour when we bleed too much within.

Remember God's expectations of the Christian church, of the believers who form the invisible body of Christ.

It was never in God's revealed plan that the Christian churches would degenerate to the point that they would begin functioning as social clubs. The fellowship of the saints that the Bible advises is never dependent upon the variety of social connections that the churches lean upon in these modern times.

The Christian church was never intended to function as a current events forum. God did not intend for a popular news magazine to serve as a textbook, providing the ramp from which a secular discussion can take off and become airborne.

You might have heard me talk about dramatics and acting, of make-believe and hypocrisy. If so, you are not surprised when I declare without equivocation that the church of Jesus Christ was never intended to become a religious theater. When we build a sanctuary and dedicate it to the worship of God, are we then obligated to provide a place in the church for entertainers to display their amateur talents?

I cannot believe that the holy, loving, sovereign God who has given us a plan of eternal salvation based on the sufferings and the death of our Lord Jesus Christ can be pleased when His church becomes any of these things.

We are neither holy enough nor wise enough to argue against the many statements in the Bible setting forth God's expectations of His people, the church, the body of Christ.

Peter reminds us that if we are believers who treasure the work of Christ on our behalf, we are a chosen generation, a royal priesthood, a holy nation, a special and peculiar people in God's sight (see 1 Peter 2:9). Paul told the Athenians that an effective and obedient believer and child of God lives and moves and has his or her being in God (see Acts 17:28).

If we are willing to confess that we have been called out of darkness to show forth the glory of Him who called us (see 1 Peter 2:9), we should also be willing to take whatever steps are necessary to fulfill our high design and calling as the New Testament church.

To do less than this is to fail utterly. It is to fail our God. It is to fail our Lord Jesus Christ who has redeemed us. It is to fail ourselves and to fail our children. It is also to miserably fail the Holy Spirit of God who has come from the heart of Jesus to do in us the works that can only be accomplished for God by a holy and sanctified people.

In this total concept of the Christian church and the members who compose it, there are two ways in which we can fail God. We can disappoint Him as a church, losing our corporate witness. Generally linked with that is our failure as individual Christians.

We look around at one another and use one of the oldest of all arguments: "Well, that kind of failure certainly could not happen here, among us."

If we are concerned and praying Christians, we will remember a pattern. When a church weakens in any generation, failing to carry out the purposes of God, it will depart from the faith altogether in the next generation.

That is how declension comes in the church. That is how apostasy comes. That is how the fundamentals of the faith are neglected. That is how the liberal and uncertain views concerning sound Christian doctrine surface.

It is a serious and tragic matter that a church can actually fail. The point of failure will come when it is no longer a Christian church. The believers who remain will know that the glory has departed.

In Israel's days of journeying, God gave the visible cloud by day and the fire by night as a witness and an evidence of His glory and constant protection. If God was still giving the same signals of His abiding Presence, I wonder how many churches would have the approving cloud by day and fire by night.

If you have any spiritual perception at all, I need not state that in our generation and in every community, large or small, there are churches existing merely as monuments of what they used to be. The glory has departed. The witness of God and of salvation and of eternal life is now just an uncertain sound. The monument is there, but the church has failed.

God does not expect us to give up, to give in, to accept the church as it is and to condone what is happening. He expects His believing children to measure the church against the standards and the blessings promised in the Word of God. Then, with love and reverence and prayer and in the leading of the Spirit of God, we will quietly and patiently endeavor to align the church with the Word of God.

When this begins to happen and the Word of God is given its place of priority, the presence of the Holy Spirit will again begin to glow in the church. That is what my heart longs to see.

Now, the second thing is the matter of individuals who are failing God.

God has had His own purposes in the creation of every man and every woman. God wants us to know the new birth from above. He wants us to know the meaning of our salvation. He wants us to be filled with His Spirit. He wants us to know the meaning of worship. He wants us to reflect the glory of the One who has called us into His marvelous light.

If we fail in this respect, then it would have been better had we never been born! The facts are plain: There is no turning back. After we are born from above, there is no turning back. We are responsible; we are accountable. How utterly tragic to be a barren fig tree, having the outward show of leaves and growth but never producing any fruit! (see Matthew 21:19). How terrible to know that God intended us to mirror His beautiful light and to have to confess that we are shattered and useless, reflecting nothing!

Be sure we will be aware of our loss, my friend. We will be aware of it. The most startling and frightful thing about us as human beings is the eternal consciousness that God has given us. It is an awareness, a consciousness, a sensitivity given us by God Himself. It is a gift to humanity—an awareness, an ability to feel.

If we had not been given such an awareness, nothing would harm us for we would never be aware of it.

Hell would not be hell if it were not for the awareness God has given men and women. If humans were just to sleep through hell, hell certainly would not be hell.

My Christian brother or sister, thank God always for the blessed gifts of sensitivity and conscience and human choice He has given you. Are you being faithful as a Christian believer where He has placed you?

If God has called you out of darkness into His light, you should be worshipping Him. If He has shown you that you are to show forth the excellencies, the virtues, the beauties of the Lord who has called you, then you should be humbly and gladly worshipping Him with the radiance and the blessing of the Holy Spirit in your life.

It is sad that we humans do not always function joyfully for God in the place He has marked out for us. We may even allow trifling things and minor incidents to disturb our fellowship with God and our spiritual witness for Him who is our Savior.

I once had an opportunity to preach in another pulpit, and after the service I was seated in a restaurant with the pastor. A man came by our table with his wife, and they stopped for a moment to talk.

"I enjoyed hearing you today, Mr. Tozer," he said. "It was like old times."

There were tears in his eyes and a softness in his voice as he recalled a minor incident in our church life years before. "I just foolishly walked out, and today was a reminder of what I have been missing," he said. He then excused himself and the couple bade us good-bye.

The man was fully aware of the consequences of poor choices and snap judgments apart from the leading of God's Spirit. I know very well that he was not talking about my sermon or my preaching. He was talking about faithfulness to the Word of God. He was talking about the sweet and satisfying fellowship among those who love the Lord. He was talking about the loss of something intrinsic and beautiful that only comes to us in our obedience to God's revealed truth.

There is no limit to what God can do through us if we are His yielded and purified people, worshipping and showing forth His glory and His faithfulness.

We must have an awareness, also, of what sin and un-

cleanness are doing all around us. Sin does not recognize
any kind of borders or limits. Sin does not operate exclu-
sively in the ghettos. Wherever you are, in the suburbs or
in the country, sin is sin. And wherever there is sin, the
devil rages and demons are abroad.

In this kind of a sinful world, what are you doing with
the spiritual light and awareness God has given you?
Where do you stand with God in your friendships, in
your pleasures, in the complexities of your day-to-day
life?

The psychologists have been telling us for some time
now that we will not have so many problems if we can just
get to the place where we do not let our religion "bother"
us. We are told we can dispel most of our personal problems by shedding our guilt complexes.

I am thankful that God has made us with an eternal
awareness, and that He knows how to lay the proper care
and concern upon us.

People call on me for spiritual guidance and coun-
seling. But I can do little for them. When a person has
come to the place of submission and obedience, God has
promised that He will give that person all the comfort he
or she needs.

After my arrival in Toronto, a cultured, attractive
young woman made an appointment to see me in my office. When she came, we talked for a few moments to get
acquainted, and then she came to the point. She said she
was troubled about her homosexual relations with her
roommate. She told me she had already talked with other
professionals about this. I had the distinct impression she
hoped I would assure her that what she was doing was
permissible in our day.

Instead, I faced her squarely. "Young woman," I said,

"you are guilty of sodomy, and God is not going to give you any approval or comfort until you turn from your known sin and seek His forgiveness and cleansing."

"I guess I needed to hear that," she admitted.

As a Christian minister and counselor, there was no way that I could console and comfort that girl and ease and soften the pain of guilt she was experiencing within her being. She would have to endure it until the moment of decision when she would confess her sin and plunge by faith into that cleansing fountain filled with blood from Immanuel's veins.

That is the remedy, that is the comfort and the necessary strength God has promised to those whose awareness and sensitivity lead them to repentance and forgiveness and wholeness.

God assures us in many ways that His worshipping people will be a purified people, a people delighting in the spiritual disciplines of a life pleasing to God.

No person who has found the blessings of purity and joy in the Holy Spirit can ever be defeated. No church that has discovered the delight and satisfaction of adoring worship that springs automatically from love and obedience to God can ever perish.

CHAPTER 9

THE NORMAL CHRISTIAN WORSHIPS GOD

God, who at sundry times and in divers manners spake in time past unto the fathers by the prophets,

Hath in these last days spoken unto us by his Son, whom he hath appointed heir of all things, by whom also he made the worlds;

Who being the brightness of his glory, and the express image of his person, and upholding all things by the word of his power, when he had by himself purged our sins, sat down on the right hand of the Majesty on high:

Being made so much better than the angels, as he hath by inheritance obtained a more excellent name than they.

But unto the Son he saith, Thy throne, O God, is for ever and ever: a sceptre of righteousness is the sceptre of thy kingdom.

Thou hast loved righteousness, and hated iniquity; therefore God, even thy God, hath anointed thee with the oil of gladness above thy fellows.

And, Thou, Lord, in the beginning hast laid the foundation of the earth; and the heavens are the works of thine hands:

They shall perish; but thou remainest; and they all shall wax old as doth a garment;

And as a vesture shalt thou fold them up, and they shall be changed: but thou art the same, and thy years shall not fail. (Hebrews 1:1–4, 8–12)

What kind of a Christian should be considered a normal Christian?" That question deserves more discussion than it currently is arousing.

Some people claim to be normal Christians when actually they mean they are nominal Christians. My old dictionary gives this definition as one of the meanings of the word *nominal*: Existing in name only; not real or actual; hence so small, slight, or the like, as to be hardly worth the name.

With that as a definition, those who know they are Christians in name only should never make the pretention of being "normal" Christians.

Is the Lord Jesus Christ your most precious treasure in this world? If so, you can count yourself among normal Christians.

Is the moral beauty which is found only in Jesus Christ constantly drawing you to praise and worship? If so, you are indeed among those whom God's Word identifies as normal, believing, practicing Christians.

But I can almost anticipate an objection. If someone is that delighted and that occupied with the person of Jesus Christ, is he or she not an extremist rather than a normal Christian?

Have professing Christians really come to that time in their humanistic and secularistic leanings that they can sincerely deny that loving Jesus Christ with all their heart and soul and strength is normal Christianity? We must not be reading and studying the same Bible!

How can anyone profess to be a follower and a disciple of Jesus Christ and not be overwhelmed by His attributes? These divine attributes attest that He is indeed Lord of all, completely worthy of our worship and praise.

As Christians we like to say that we have "crowned Him Lord of all," but we find it difficult to express what we really mean.

I have always been interested in the phrasing of one of our great hymns:

Lord of all being, throned afar,
Thy glory flames from sun and star;
The Normal Christian Worships God a
Center and soul of every sphere,
Yet to each loving heart how near.

The Lord of all being is far more than the Lord of all beings. He is the Lord of all actual existence. He is the Lord of all kinds of being—spiritual being, natural being, physical being. Therefore, when we rightly worship Him, we encompass all being.

When young people begin to comprehend this truth of the highest position and stature in the universe accorded to Jesus Christ as Lord of all, they also begin to sense the importance of His call to a lifetime of loving service.

Many young people give themselves wholly to science and some to technology and some to philosophy or to music or the arts. When we worship the Lord Jesus Christ, however, we embrace and encompass all possible sciences and philosophies and arts. This is our answer to those in other religious backgrounds who are willing to accept that Jesus was a man but who do not accept His claim to be One with the Father as the eternal Son of God.

These other religionists contend that when we give

worship to the man Jesus Christ, we are guilty of idolatry, because we, too, have confessed that He was man. We do believe that Jesus came among us as the Son of Man, but we believe the entire record. That record informs us He was the only begotten of the Father. Thus Jesus was also God.

By the mystery of the Incarnation, Jesus Christ was fully united with men and women of the human race. The eternal plan was not to bring God down to man's level but for the Son to take humanity up into God. Thus we are to be joined in the beauty and wonder of the theanthropic union—God and man in one.

The synopsis of this unique mystery involving God and man is just this: Whatever God is, Christ is. When you are worshipping the Lord Jesus, you are not displeasing the Father. Jesus is the Lord of all being, and He is the Lord of all life.

The Apostle John has told us plainly in his first epistle that none of us would know anything about the meaning of life if Jesus had not come forth from the Father to show us the true meaning of eternal life. But He came, and as a result, John assures us, "Our fellowship is with the Father, and with His Son Jesus Christ" (1 John 1:3).

The fact that Christ is now the fountain of life for redeemed and worshipping men and women was expressed simply in the meaningful hymn "Jesus Lover of My Soul," by Charles Wesley:

> Plenteous grace with Thee is found,
> Grace to cover all my sin;
> Let the healing streams abound;
> Make and keep me pure within.
> Thou of life the Fountain art,
> Freely let me take of Thee;

Spring Thou up within my heart,
Rise to all eternity.

We know that there are many kinds of life, and we may be assured that Jesus is the Lord of all kinds of life. In the spring, we watch the new, eager buds on the trees and shrubs. They are ready to push themselves out and extend themselves into the blooming patterns of floral life.

Soon we expect to see the birds return. I do not forgive the birds too easily—they are such fair-weather friends. On the dark and stormy days when we need them the most, they are in Florida. But they return each spring, expressing their own kind of life as they warble.

We begin to see the rabbits and the other animals. They have their own kind of life. Christ is Creator and Lord of them all. Beyond these manifestations of life is the intellectual life, for instance—the life of imagination and dreams.

We know something also of the spiritual life. "God is a Spirit and they that worship him must worship him in spirit and in truth" (John 4:24). God's eternal Son is our Lord. He is the Lord of angels, and He is the Lord of the cherubim and seraphim. He is the Lord of every kind of life—this same Jesus.

In our day it is important that we find out Jesus Christ is the Lord of all wisdom and the Lord of all righteousness.

The sum total of the deep and eternal wisdom of the ages lies in Jesus Christ as a treasure hidden away. There is no kind of true wisdom that cannot be found within Him. All the deep eternal purposes of God reside in Him because His perfect wisdom enables Him to plan far ahead. All history becomes the slow development of His eternal purposes.

God in His wisdom is making evil men as well as good men, adverse things as well as favorable things work for the bringing forth of His glory in the day when all shall be fulfilled in Him.

The Scriptures give us many delightful concepts of the manner in which Christ is the Lord of all righteousness.

Righteousness is not a word that is easily acceptable to lost men and women in a lost world. Someone will say, "Oh, I will be satisfied if I can just get my hands on a good book dealing with ethics." Outside of the Word of God, there is no book or treatise that can give us a satisfying answer about righteousness because the only One who is Lord of all righteousness is our Lord Jesus Christ Himself. A scepter of righteousness is the scepter of His kingdom. He is the only One in all the universe who has perfectly loved righteousness and hated iniquity.

In the Old Testament period, there was a picture of righteousness in the shadows of the temple system of worship. The high priest was instructed to enter into the Holy of Holies once each year to offer the sacrifices (see Leviticus 16:32–34). He wore a miter on his forehead, and the Hebrew words engraved on the miter would be translated in English, "Holiness unto the Lord" (see Exodus 28:36–38). Our great High Priest and Mediator is the righteous and holy One—Jesus Christ, our risen Lord. He is not only righteous, He is the Lord of all righteousness (see Hebrews 9:11–12).

Then, too, He is the Lord of all mercy. Who else would establish His kingdom upon rebels—rebels whom He himself has redeemed and in whom He has renewed a right spirit?

Think with me about beauty—and this One who is the Lord of all beauty. We know by our own reactions and enjoyment that God has deposited something within the human being that is capable of understanding and appreciating beauty. God has put within us the love of harmonious forms, the love and appreciation of color and beautiful sounds.

What many of us do not understand is that all beautiful things, so pleasant to the eyes and ears, are only the external counterparts of a deeper and more enduring beauty—that which we call moral beauty.

In relation to Jesus Christ, it has been the uniqueness and the perfection of His moral beauty that has charmed even those who claimed to be His enemies throughout the centuries of history. We do not have any record of Hitler saying anything against the moral perfections of Jesus. One of the great philosophers, Nietzsche, himself an instrument of anti-Christian forces in this world, died finally beating his forehead on the floor and moaning, "That man Jesus I love. I don't like Paul."

Nietzsche objected to Paul's theology of justification and salvation by faith, but he was strangely moved within by the perfections of moral beauty found in the life and character of Jesus, the Christ, the Lord of all beauty.

We see this perfection in Jesus, but when we look closely at this world system and society, we see the terrible and ugly scars of sin. Sin has obscenely scarred and defaced this world, making it inharmonious and unsymmetrical and ugly, so that even hell is filled with ugliness.

If you love beautiful things, you had better stay out of hell, for hell will be the quintessence of all that is morally ugly and obscene. Hell will be the ugliest place in all of creation. When rough-talking men say that something is "as ugly as hell," they employ a proper and valid comparison. Hell is that reality against which all ugliness is measured.

That is the negative picture. Thank God for the positive promise and prospect of heaven's being the place of supreme beauty. Heaven is the place of harmonious numbers. Heaven is the place of loveliness. The One who is all beautiful is there. He is the Lord of all beauty.

My brother or sister, earth lies between all that is ugly in hell and all that is beautiful in heaven. As long as we are living in this world, we will have to consider the extremes. Light and darkness. Beauty and ugliness. Much that is good and much that is bad. The things that are pleasant and those that are tragic and harsh.

Why? Because of the sense in which our world lies halfway between heaven's beauty and hell's ugliness.

Against that background let me report a person who called me to ask this question: "Mr. Tozer, do you think a person who is really a Christian can hurt another Christian?"

I was forced to say, "Yes, I think so."

Why is it that a man can be on his knees one day, praying earnestly, and the next day be guilty of offending or injuring another Christian?

I think the answer is because we are halfway between heaven and hell. It is because the shadows and light fall upon us.

The best answer is that we are being saved out of all of this. The Lord of all beauty is saving His people from the ugliness of sin. Our Lord Jesus Christ came to this ugly, selfish, violent world that He might save us and deliver us to a beautiful heaven.

We will never be able to comprehend the awful, terrible price the Lord of all beauty paid to gain our redemption. The prophet said of the Messiah to come, "There is no beauty [in Him] that we should desire him" (Isaiah 53:2). I do not believe the artists have given a proper concept of Jesus the man. They paint Him as a pretty man with a tender, feminine face. They ignore the statement that "there was no beauty that we should desire him."

Jesus was fully one of us, a strong Man among men. He apparently was so much like His disciples that Judas Iscariot had to make a special arrangement to earn his thirty pieces of silver. "Whomsoever I shall kiss, that same is he" (Mark 14:44).

We might well say that when the eternal Son had taken on the form of a man, only His soul was beautiful. Only when He was suddenly transfigured on the mount did "his face did shine as the sun, and his raiment was white as the light" (Matthew 17:2). Only then did His closest disciples really see how beautiful He was. While He walked among men, His perfect beauty was veiled.

There is an effective illustration in the types and figures of the Old Testament reminding us of the adornments of grace and beauty that will mark the believing body of Christ, the church, being prepared as the bride awaiting the heavenly Bridegroom. It is the memorable story of Isaac and Rebekah in Genesis 24. Abraham sent his trusted servant to his former homeland to select a bride for Isaac. Of course, Rebekah passed all of the tests that Abraham's servant had posed. There is no statement concerning Rebekah's beauty, but presumably she was beautiful.

The adornment of her beauty consisted of the jewels and the raiment that came as gifts of love from the bridegroom whom she had not yet seen.

It is a reminder of what God is doing in our midst right now. Abraham typifies God the Father; Isaac, our

Lord Jesus Christ, the heavenly Bridegroom. The servant who went with his gifts into the far country to claim a bride for Isaac speaks well of the Holy Spirit, our Teacher and Comforter.

I ask, what is our real beauty as we are called out one by one to take our places by faith in the body of Christ to await His coming? God has not left this to chance. He gives us one by one the beauties, the gifts, the graces of the Holy Spirit, typified only imperfectly by those jewels and gems that the servant bestowed on behalf of Isaac. Thus we are being prepared, and when we meet Jesus Christ as our coming Lord and King, our adornment will be our God-given graces and gifts. By that means it will be possible for us to stand with the One who is the Lord of all beauty!

If you do not know Him and worship Him, if you do not long to reside where He is, if you have never known wonder and ecstasy in your soul because of His crucifixion and resurrection, your claim of Christianity is unfounded. It cannot be related to the true Christian life and experience at all.

Meanwhile, I believe that we as Christians must become willing to allow every ugly thing in our lives to be crucified. We must indeed worship the Lord of all beauty in spirit and in truth. This is not a popular thing, for so many Christians insist that they must be entertained while they are being edified.

I have long been a student of the life and ministry of Albert B. Simpson, founder of The Christian and Missionary Alliance. I pass on to you his warning that we may become so enamored of God's good gifts that we fail to worship the Giver.

Dr. Simpson was once invited to preach at a Bible

conference in England, on the assigned topic, "Sanctification." When he arrived, he discovered that he was to be
on the platform with two other Bible teachers. All three
of them had been given the same topic—"Sanctification."

The first speaker used his time in making clear his position that sanctification meant eradication. "The sanctified person has had his or her old carnal nature removed,
as you would remove a weed from your garden—eradi-
cated."

The second speaker arose and set forth his view that
sanctification meant the suppression of the old nature.
"The 'old man' will always be there," he said, "and your
victory is to sit on the lid and keep him down and beat
him at his own game. He must be suppressed."

That was not an easy situation for Dr. Simpson, sched-
uled to be the third and final speaker.

He told the audience that he could only present Christ
Himself as God's answer. "Jesus Christ is your Sanctifier,
your sanctification, your all and in all. God wants you
to get your eyes away from the gifts, the formulas, the
techniques. He wants your gaze to be on the Giver, Christ
Himself. He is your Lord; worship Him."

That is a wonderful word for those who would worship rightly.

Once it was the blessing;
Now it is the Lord.

CHAPTER 10

IF YOU WORSHIP ON SUNDAY, WHAT HAPPENS ON MONDAY?

Now Moses kept the flock of Jethro his father in law, the priest of Midian: and he led the flock to the backside of the desert, and came to the mountain of God, even to Horeb.

And the angel of the LORD appeared unto him in a flame of fire out of the midst of a bush: and he looked, and, behold, the bush burned with fire, and the bush was not consumed.

And Moses said, I will now turn aside, and see this great sight, why the bush is not burnt.

And when the LORD saw that he turned aside to see, God called unto him out of the midst of the bush, and said, Moses, Moses. And he said, Here am I.

And he said, Draw not nigh hither: put off thy shoes from off thy feet, for the place whereon thou standest is holy ground.

Moreover he said, I am the God of thy father, the God of Abraham, the God of Isaac, and the God of Jacob. And Moses hid his face; for he was afraid to look upon God. (Exodus 3:1–6)

Do you quietly bow your head in reverence when you step into the average gospel church?

I am not surprised if your answer is no.

There is grief in my spirit when I go into the average church, for we have become a generation rapidly losing all sense of divine sacredness in our worship. Many whom we have raised in our churches no longer think in terms of reverence—which seems to indicate they doubt that God's Presence is there.

In too many of our churches, you can detect the attitude that anything goes. It is my assessment that losing the awareness of God in our midst is a loss too terrible ever to be appraised.

Much of the blame must be placed on the growing acceptance of a worldly secularism that seems much more appealing in our church circles than any hungering or thirsting for the spiritual life that pleases God. We secularize God, we secularize the gospel of Christ and we secularize worship.

No great and spiritually powerful man of God is going to come out of such a church. No great spiritual movement of believing prayer and revival is going to come out of such a church. If God is to be honored and revered and truly worshipped, He may have to sweep us away and start somewhere else.

There is a necessity for true worship among us. If God is who He says He is and if we are the believing people of God we claim to be, we must worship Him. I do not believe that we will ever truly delight in the adoring worship of God if we have never met Him in personal, spiritual experience through the new birth from above, wrought by the Holy Spirit of God Himself!

We have such smooth, almost secularized ways of

talking people into the kingdom of God that we can no longer find men and women willing to seek God through the crisis of encounter. When we bring them into our churches, they have no idea of what it means to love and worship God because, in the route through which we have brought them, there has been no personal encounter, no personal crisis, no need of repentance—only a Bible verse with a promise of forgiveness.

Oh, how I wish I could adequately set forth the glory of that One who is worthy to be the object of our worship! I do believe that if our new converts—the babes in Christ—could be made to see His thousand attributes and even partially comprehend His being, they would become faint with a yearning desire to worship and honor and acknowledge Him, now and forever.

I know that many discouraged Christians do not truly believe in God's sovereignty. In that case we are not filling our role as the humble and trusting followers of God and His Christ.

And yet, that is why Christ Jesus came into our world. The old theologians called it theanthropism—the union of the divine and human natures in Christ. This is a great mystery, and I stand in awe before it. I take off my shoes and kneel before this burning bush, this mystery I do not understand.

The theanthropy is the mystery of God and man united in one person—not two persons, but two natures.

So, the nature of God and the nature of man are united in this One who is our Lord Jesus Christ. All that is God and all that is man are in Christ fused eternally and inextricably.

Consider the experience of Moses in the desert as he beheld the fire that burned in the bush without consuming it. Moses had no hesitation in kneeling before the bush and worshipping God. Moses was not worshipping a bush; it was God and His glory dwelling in the bush that Moses worshipped.

That is an imperfect illustration, for when the fire departed from that bush it was a bush again.

But this Man, Christ Jesus, is eternally the Son. In the fullness of this mystery, there has never been any departure, except for that awful moment when Jesus cried, "My God, my God, why hast thou forsaken me?" (Matthew 27:46). The Father turned His back for a moment when the Son took on Himself that putrifying mass of our sin and guilt, dying on the cross not for His own sin, but for ours.

The deity and the humanity never parted. And to this day they remain united in that one Man. When we kneel before Him and say, "My Lord and my God, Thy throne, O God, is forever and ever," we are talking to God.

I think the prophets of God saw farther into the centuries and into the mysteries of God than we can with our great modern telescopes and electronic means of measuring light-years and planets and galaxies.

The prophets saw the Lord our God. They saw Him in His beauty, and they tried to describe Him.

They described Him as radiantly beautiful and fair, a winsome being. They said that He was royal and that He was gracious. They described Him as a majestic being; and yet they noted His meekness. They saw Him as righteous and filled with truth. They tried to describe the manner of His love, with its gladness and joy and fragrance.

When the prophets try to describe for me the attributes, the graces, the worthiness of the God who appeared to them and dealt with them, I feel that I can kneel down and follow their admonition: "He is thy Lord—worship thou Him."

He is fair and He is kingly, yet He is gracious in a sense that takes nothing away from His majesty.

He is meek, but it is the kind of meekness that likewise takes nothing away from His majesty.

The meekness and the majesty of Jesus. I wish I could write a hymn about that or compose music about it. Where else can you find majesty and meekness united?

The meekness was His humanity. The majesty was His deity. You find them everlastingly united in Him. So meek that he nursed at His mother's breast, cried like any baby and needed all the human care that every child needs.

But He was also God, and in His majesty He stood before Herod and before Pilate. When He returns, coming down from the sky, it will be in His majesty, the majesty of God. Yet it will also be in the majesty of the Man who is God.

This is our Lord Jesus Christ. Before His foes, He stands in majesty. Before His friends, He comes in meekness.

It is given to men and women to choose—a person may have either side. If he does not want the meek side of Jesus, he will come to know the majestic side.

On earth, the children came to Him. The sick and the sinful came to Him. The devil-possessed man came to Him. Those who knew their needs came from everywhere and touched Him, finding Him so meek that His power went out to them and healed them.

When He appears to men again, it will be in majesty. In His kingly majesty He will deal with the pride and conceit and self-sufficiency of mankind, for the Bible says that every knee will bow and every tongue will confess that He is Lord and King.

To really know Him is to love and worship Him.

As God's people, we are so often confused that we could be known as God's poor, stumbling, bumbling people. That must be true of a great number of us for we always think of worship as something we do when we go to church.

We call it God's house. We have dedicated it to Him. So we continue with the confused idea that it must be the only place where we can worship Him.

We come to the Lord's house, made out of brick and wood and lined with carpeting. We are used to hearing a call to worship: "The Lord is in His holy temple—let us all kneel before Him."

That is on Sunday, and that is in church. Very nice!

But Monday morning comes soon. The Christian layman goes to his office. The Christian schoolteacher goes to the classroom. The Christian mother is busy with duties in the home.

On Monday, as we go about our different duties and tasks, are we aware of the Presence of God? The Lord desires still to be in His holy temple, wherever we are. He wants the continuing love and delight and worship of His children, wherever we work.

Is it not a beautiful thing for a businessman to enter his office on Monday morning with an inner call to worship: "The Lord is in my office—let all the world be silent before Him."

If you cannot worship the Lord in the midst of your responsibilities on Monday, it is not very likely that you were worshipping on Sunday!

Actually, none of us has the ability to fool God. Therefore, if we are so engaged in our Saturday pursuits that we are far from His presence and far from a sense of worship on Saturday, we are not in very good shape to worship Him on Sunday.

I guess many people have an idea that they have God in a box. He is just in the church sanctuary, and when we leave and drive toward home, we have a rather faint, homesick feeling that we are leaving God in the big box.

You know that is not true, but what are you doing about it?

God is not confined to a building any more than He is confined to your car or your home or the office where you work.

Paul's earnest exhortation to the Corinthian Christians is just as valid for our lives today as it was when he expressed it:

> *Know ye not that ye are the temple of God, and that the Spirit of God dwelleth in you? If any man defile the temple of God, him shall God destroy; for the temple of God is holy, which temple ye are.* (1 Corinthians 3:16–17)

If you do not know the presence of God in your office, your factory, your home, then God is not in the church when you attend.

I became a Christian when I was a young man working in one of the tire factories in Akron, Ohio. I remember my work there. I remember my worship there too. I had plenty of worshipful tears in my eyes. No one ever asked me about them, but I would not have hesitated to explain them.

You can learn to use certain skills until they are automatic. I became so skillful that I could do my work, and then I could worship God even while my hands were busy.

I have come to believe that when we are worshipping—and it could be right at the drill in the factory—if the love of God is in us and the Spirit of God is breathing praise within us, all the musical instruments in heaven are suddenly playing in full support.

Well, it is my experience that our total lives, our entire attitude as persons, must be toward the worship of God.

What is there in you that strives to worship God? Faith, love, obedience, loyalty, conduct of life—all of these strive in you to worship God. If there is anything within you that refuses to worship, there is nothing within you, then, that worships God very well.

You are not worshipping God as you should if you have departmentalized your life so that some areas worship and other parts do not worship.

This can be a great delusion—that worship only happens in church or in the midst of a dangerous storm or in the presence of some unusual and sublime beauty of nature around us. I have been with some fellows who became very spiritual when they stood on the breathtaking curve of a steep mountain cliff!

Occasionally we are in some situation like that and a person begins to yell, "Hooray for Jesus!"—or some other corny expression.

My brother or sister, if we are believing children of God in whom the Holy Spirit nurtures continual joy, delight and wonder, we will not need a storm on the mountain to show us how glorious our Lord really is.

It is a delusion to think that because we suddenly feel expansive and poetic in the presence of the storm or stars or space, that we are spiritual. I need only remind you that drunkards or tyrants or criminals can have those "sublime" feelings too. Let us not imagine that they constitute worship.

I can offer no worship wholly pleasing to God if I know that I am harboring elements in my life that are displeasing to Him. I cannot truly and joyfully worship God on Sunday and not worship Him on Monday. I cannot worship God with a glad song on Sunday and then knowingly displease Him in my business dealings on Monday and Tuesday.

I repeat my view of worship—no worship is wholly pleasing to God until there is nothing in me displeasing to God.

Is that a view that seems very discouraging to you?

Let me say that if you listen to me long enough, you will receive some encouragement in the Spirit, but I have never had an inclination within me to encourage people in the flesh.

I have never had very much faith in people—as people. I do respect the good intentions that people have. I know they mean well. But in the flesh they cannot fulfill their good intentions. That is because we are sinners and we are all in a predicament—until we find the source of victory and joy and blessing in Jesus Christ.

There is nothing in either of us that can be made good until Jesus Christ comes and changes us—until He lives in us and unites our nature with God, the Father Almighty. Not until then can we call ourselves good.

That is why I say that your worship must be total. It must involve the whole you. That is why you must prepare to worship God, and that preparation is not always pleasant. There may be revolutionary changes that must take place in your life.

If there is to be true and blessed worship, some things in your life must be destroyed, eliminated. The gospel of

Jesus Christ is certainly positive and constructive. But it must be destructive in some areas, dealing with and destroying certain elements that cannot remain in a life pleasing to God.

There have always been professing Christians who argue: "I worship in the name of Jesus." They seem to believe that worship of God is a formula. They seem to think there is a kind of magic in saying the name of Jesus.

Study the Bible carefully with the help of the Holy Spirit, and you will find that the name and the nature of Jesus are one. It is not enough to know how to spell Jesus' name. If we have come to be like Him in nature, if we have come to the place of being able to ask in accordance with His will, He will give us the good things we desire and need. We do not worship in name only. We worship God as the result of a birth from above in which God has been pleased to give us more than a name. He has given us a nature transformed.

Peter expressed that truth this way: "Whereby are given unto us exceeding great and precious promises: that by these ye might be partakers of the divine nature, having escaped the corruption that is in the world through lust" (2 Peter 1:4).

Why should we delude ourselves about pleasing God in worship? If I live like a worldly and carnal tramp all day and then find myself in a time of crisis at midnight, how do I pray to a God who is holy? How do I address the One who has asked me to worship Him in spirit and in truth? Do I get on my knees and call on the name of Jesus because I believe there is some magic in that name?

If I am still the same worldly, carnal tramp, I will be disappointed and disillusioned. If I am not living in the true meaning of His name and His nature, I cannot properly pray in that name. If I am not living in His nature, I cannot rightly pray in that nature.

How can we hope to worship God acceptably when these evil elements remain in our natures undisciplined, uncorrected, unpurged, unpurified? Even granted that a man with evil ingredients in his nature might manage through some part of himself to worship God half-acceptably. But what kind of a way is that in which to live and continue?

"I want to dwell in your thoughts," God has been saying. "Make your thoughts a sanctuary in which I can dwell."

I do not have to do something wrong to feel blistering conviction and repent. I can lose fellowship with God, lose the keen sense of His presence and lose the blessing of spiritual victory by thinking wrong.

I have found that God will not dwell in spiteful and polluted thoughts. He will not dwell in lustful and covetous thoughts. He will not dwell in proud and selfish thoughts.

God tells us to make a sanctuary of our thoughts in which He can dwell. He treasures our pure and loving thoughts, our meek and charitable and kindly thoughts. These are the thoughts like His own.

As God dwells in your thoughts, you will be worshipping, and God will be accepting. He will be smelling the incense of your high intention even when the cares of life are intense and activity is all around you.

If God knows that your intention is to worship Him with every part of your being, He has promised to cooperate with you. On His side is the love and grace, the promises and the atonement, the constant help and the presence of the Holy Spirit.

On your side there is determination, seeking, yielding, believing. Your heart becomes a chamber, a sanctuary, a shrine in which there may be continuous, unbroken fellowship and communion with God. Your worship rises to God moment by moment.

Two of Spurgeon's greatest sermons were about "God in the Silence" and "God in the Storm." The heart that knows God can find God anywhere. I surely join with Spurgeon in the truth that a person filled with the Spirit of God, a person who has met God in a living encounter, can know the joy of worshipping Him, whether in the silences of life or in the storms of life. There really is no argument. We know what God wants us to be. He wants us to be worshippers!

WORSHIP:
THE MISSING JEWEL
IN THE EVANGELICAL CHURCH

ACCEPTABLE WORSHIP

WORSHIP:
THE NORMAL EMPLOYMENT
OF MORAL BEINGS

In 1961 A.W. Tozer spoke to the pastors of the Associated Gospel Churches of Canada. These three messages on worship were then edited by Tozer for the organization's publication, *The Advance*. In 1965 they were reprinted as a series in *The Alliance Witness* (now *Alliance Life*), the magazine Tozer edited from 1950 until his death in 1963. The series has been in print as a booklet and in several languages ever since.

We offer the booklet here, in its entirety, as a companion to *Whatever Happened to Worship?*, both of which reveal Tozer's strong convictions about worship that are so timely still today.

"We are saved to worship God. All that Christ has done for us in the past and all that He is doing now lead to this one end...." (From *Whatever Happened to Worship?*)

Worship:
The Missing Jewel
in the Evangelical Church

In the Psalms you hear a rapturous call to worship. They answer that famous question put to us by the Presbyterians: "What is the chief end of man?" The answer to that question is what I want to talk about now and say to you that we were created, and after the Fall redeemed, that we might be worshippers of the Most High God.

God never acts without purpose—never. People act without purpose. I feel that a great deal of what we do in the church today is purposeless. But God never acts without a purpose. Intellect is an attribute of the deity. God has intellect, and this means that God thinks; and so God never does anything without an intelligent purpose. Nothing in this world is without meaning.

God put the universe together with a purpose, and there isn't a single useless thing anywhere; not any spare parts; everything fits into everything else. God made it like that. Science of course deals with the relation of things and their effect upon each other. But the plain people, the simple people, the people who would rather believe than to know, and who would rather worship than to discover—they have a simpler and a more beautiful view of the world. They say that in the beginning God created the heavens and the earth, and that God made everything and put it in its place and gave it meaning and purpose and a task to fulfill in relation to all other things which He also made.

But God saw that the world wasn't complete, so as the poem has it, this great God who threw the stars into the sky and made the sun and holds all the universe in His hand, this great God stooped down by the riverbank and took a piece of clay and, like a mammy bending over her baby, He worked on this clay until it became a man and into it He blew the breath of life and it became a living soul. Amen! Amen! That's what we believe. We don't think about it in quite such a physical way as that, but we believe that God in His intelligence created the universe with intelligent purpose back of it.

And when we say this, we know very well that some philosophies hold otherwise. But we pay no attention. We begin with gentle dogmatism. Now I use the word *dogmatism* because I want to be dogmatic about what I'm saying. But I use the word *gentle* because I don't want to become offensively dogmatic. I want to be gently dogmatic. I believe what I'm saying. I believe it completely. I believe it with sufficient emphasis that I control my life by it. It has been the reason I've lived and it's the reason, if the Lord tarry, I can die boldly.

Now, these plain people of whom I speak believe that God created things for a purpose. He created the flowers, for instance, to be beautiful; He created birds to sing; He created the trees to bear fruit and the beasts to feed and clothe mankind. And in so saying, these people affirm what the Holy Scriptures and Moses and the prophets and the apostles and saints since the world began have all said. God made man for a purpose and that purpose is given by the catechism; the answer is, "To glorify God and to enjoy Him forever." God made us to be worshippers. That was the purpose of God in bringing us into the world.

I believe there is good sound reasoning back of all this. I believe that He created man out of no external necessity. I believe it was an internal necessity. God, being the God He was and is, and being infinitely perfect and infinitely beautiful and infinitely glorious and infinitely admirable and infinitely loving, out of His own inward necessity had to have some creature that was capable of admiring Him and loving Him and knowing Him. So God made man in His own image; in the image and likeness of God made He him; and He made him as near to being like Himself as it was possible for the creature to be like the Creator. The most godlike thing in the universe is the soul of man.

The reason God made man in His image was that he might appreciate God and admire and adore and worship; so that God might not be a picture, so to speak, hanging in a gallery with nobody looking at Him. He might not be a flower that no one could smell; He might not be a star that no one could see. God made somebody to smell that flower, the lily of the valley. He wanted someone to see that glorious image. He wanted someone to see the star, so He made us and in making us, He made us to worship Him.

I'm going to give you a definition of the word *worship* as I shall use it. You'll not find this definition anywhere because I made it myself. After Webster's done the best he can for you, then a good thinker ought to make his own definition. If you don't define, you won't be understood; if you define too much, you won't be listened to, because there isn't anything so boring as a preacher who gets up and gives you a lecture on Webster; but if you don't define enough, people won't know what you mean. You'll be talking about one thing, and your audience will be hearing something else, and you might not mean the same thing at all.

I want to define *worship*, and here is where I want to be dogmatic. *Worship* means "to feel in the heart"; that's first—feel it in the heart. Now I happen to belong to that segment of the church of Christ on earth that is not afraid of the word "feeling." We went through a long deep-freeze period at the turn of the century, when people talked about "naked faith." They wanted to hang us out there like a coonskin drying on the door. And so they said, "Now, don't believe in feeling, brother; we don't believe in feeling. The only man who went by feeling was led astray; that was Isaac when he felt Jacob's arms and thought it was Esau." But they forgot the woman who felt in her body that she was healed! Remember that! A person that merely goes through the form and doesn't feel anything is not worshipping.

Worship also means to "express in some appropriate manner" what you feel. Now, expressing in some appropriate manner doesn't mean that we always all express it in the same way all the time. And it doesn't mean that you will always express your worship in the same manner. But it does mean that it will be expressed in some manner.

And what will be expressed! "A humbling but delightful sense of admiring awe and astonished wonder." It is delightful to worship God, but it is also a humbling thing; and the man who has not been humbled in the presence of God will never be a worshipper of God at all. He may be a church member who keeps the rules and obeys the discipline, and who tithes and goes to conference, but he'll never be a worshipper unless he is deeply humbled. "A humbling but delightful sense of admiring awe." There's an awesomeness about God that is missing in our day altogether; there's little sense of admiring awe in the church of Christ these days.

I like some of the things you do here in Canada very much. It probably started in a simple form and whoever did it first had a good idea—after the benediction you sit down and worship a minute. That's very good. I'm sure that for many it has become form. But when it's real it's a good thing. I see some occasionally who come in and bow their heads and worship before the service starts. Well, there's that admiration and awe. If there is no fear of God in our hearts, there can be no worship of God.

"Awesome wonder and overpowering love" in the presence of that ancient Mystery, that unspeakable Majesty, which the philosophers call the *Mysterium Tremendum*, but which we call our Father which art in heaven. Now that's my definition of worship, and that's what I'm going to mean from here on—that we are to feel something in our heart that we didn't have before we were converted; that we're going to express it in some way, and it's going to be a humbling but a most enjoyable sense of admiring awe and astonished wonder and overpowering love in the Presence of that most ancient Mystery.

An awful thing has happened to us, brethren, when we can explain the Christian faith. I am just as much afraid of evangelical rationalism as I am of liberalism; they're both heading in the same direction. In the States now we have a new school of thought that goes by various names; new evangelicalism, it's called, but it's neo-rationalism. The evangelical rationalism that tries to explain everything takes the mystery out of life and the mystery out of worship. When you have taken the mystery out, you have taken God out, for while we may be able to understand Him in some measure, we can never fully understand God. There must always be that awe upon our spirits that says, "Ah, Lord God, Thou knowest!"—that stands silent and breathless or kneels in the presence of that awful Wonder, that Mystery, that unspeakable Majesty, before whom the prophets used to fall, and before whom Peter and John and the rest of them fell down as if dead, before whom Isaiah recoiled and cried, "I am a man of unclean lips."

Now we were made to worship, but the Scriptures tell us something else again. They tell us that man fell and kept not his first estate; that he forfeited the original glory of God and failed to fulfill the creative purpose, so that he is not worshipping now in the way that God meant him to worship. All else fulfills its design; flowers are still fragrant and lilies are still beautiful and the bees still search for nectar amongst the flowers, the birds still sing with their thousand-voice choir on a summer's day, and the sun and the moon and the stars all move on their rounds doing the will of God.

And from what we can learn from the Scriptures, we believe that the seraphim and cherubim and powers and dominions are still fulfilling their design—worshipping God who created them and breathed into them the breath of life. Man alone sulks in his cave.

Man alone, with all of his brilliant intelligence, with all of his amazing, indescribable and wonderful equipment, still sulks in his cave. He is either silent, or if he opens his mouth at all, it is to boast and threaten and curse; or it's nervous, ill-considered laughter, or it's humor become big business, or it's songs without joy.

Man was made to worship God. God gave to man a harp and said, "Here above all the creatures that I have made and created, I have given you the largest harp. I put more strings on your instrument and I have given you a wider range than I have given to any other creature. You can worship Me in a manner that no other creature can." And when he sinned, man took that instrument and threw it down in the mud, and there it has lain for centuries, rusted, broken, unstrung; and man, instead of playing a harp like the angels and seeking to worship God in all of his activities, is ego centered and turns in on himself and sulks and swears and laughs and sings, but it's all without joy and without worship.

Now, God Almighty sent His Son Jesus Christ into the world for a purpose, and what was the purpose? To hear the average evangelist nowadays you'd think that we might give up tobacco; that Christ came into the world that we might escape hell; that He sent His Son into the world that when at last we get old and tired we might have some place to go. Now all of these things are true. Jesus Christ does save us from bad habits and He does redeem us from hell and He does prepare us a place in heaven; but that is not the ultimate purpose of redemption.

The purpose of God in sending His Son to die and rise and live and be at the right hand of God the Father was that He might restore to us the missing jewel, the jewel of worship; that we might come back and learn to do again that which we were created to do in the first place—worship the Lord in the beauty of holiness, to spend our time in awesome wonder and adoration of God, feeling and expressing it, and letting it get into our labors and doing nothing except as an act of worship to Almighty God through His Son Jesus Christ. I say that the greatest tragedy in the world today is that God has made man in His image and made him to worship Him, made him to play the harp of worship before the face of God day and night, but he has failed God and dropped the harp. It lies voiceless at his feet.

Without worship we go about miserable; that's why we have all the troubles we have. You wonder why young people act like such idiots. Some young people have a lot of energy and don't know what to do with it, so they go out and act like idiots; and that's why gangsters and Communists and sinners of all kinds do what they do. They are endowed by God Almighty with brilliant intelligence and an amazing store of energy, and because they don't know what to do with it, they do the wrong thing. That's why I'm not angry with people when I see them go off the deep end, because I know that they have fallen from their first estate along with Adam's brood and all of us together. They haven't been redeemed and so they have energy they don't know what to do with; they have capacity they don't know how to use. They have skills and don't know where to put them, and so they go wild, and police have to arrest sixteen-year-olds and put them in jail. If they had been taught that they came into the world in the first place to worship God and to enjoy Him forever and that when they fell, Jesus Christ came to redeem them, to make worshippers out of them, they could by the Holy Ghost and the washing of the blood be made into worshipping saints and things would be so different.

But not all young people have gone wild. I can show you young people by the scores and by the hundreds and running into the thousands who with all their exuberance have turned their eyes upon Jesus and looked full in His wonderful face; they have been redeemed, and they know why they have been created. What Plato didn't know and Pythagoras didn't know and Aristotle didn't know and what Julian Huxley doesn't know—why they were created—these simple-hearted young people know. They know why they came into the world.

That's why I believe in the deeper life. I believe that the farther on with God we go, the farther up into Christ's heart we move, the more like Christ we'll become; and the more like Christ we become, the more like God we'll become; and the more we become like Him and the nearer we are to Him, the more perfect our worship will be.

I think that God has given me a little bit of a spirit of a crusader and I am crusading where I can that Christians of all denominations and shades of theological thought might be restored again to our original purpose. We're here to be worshippers first and workers only second. We take a convert and immediately make a worker out of him. God never meant it to be so. God meant that a convert should learn to be a worshipper, and after that he can learn to be a worker. Jesus said, "Go ye into all the world, and preach the gospel" (Mark 16:15). Peter wanted to go at once but Christ said, "Don't go yet. Wait until you are endued with power" (see Acts 1:4). Power for service! Yes, but that's only half of it; maybe that's only one-tenth of it. The other nine-tenths are that the Holy Ghost may restore to us again the spirit of worship. Out of enraptured, admiring, adoring, worshipping souls, then, God does His work. The work done by a worshipper will have eternity in it.

ACCEPTABLE WORSHIP

✳

God wants us to worship Him. He doesn't need us, for He couldn't be a self-sufficient God and need anything or anybody, but He wants us. When Adam sinned, it was not he who cried, "God, where art Thou?" It was God who cried, "Adam, where art thou?" (see Genesis 3:9).

Paul, in writing to the Thessalonians, referred to the time when Christ shall come to be glorified in the saints and admired by all them that believe He wants to be glorified (see 2 Thessalonians 1:10). Those are a few proof texts in addition to the one I have read from the Psalms, but more convincing than any proof text is the full import and drift of the Scriptures. The whole substance of the Bible teaches that God wants us to worship Him.

Now, there are good, sound, theological and philosophical reasons for this. But while God wants us to worship Him, we cannot worship Him just any way we will. The One who made us to worship Him has decreed how we shall worship Him. He accepts only the worship that He Himself has decreed.

I want to speak of some kinds of worship that God has ruled out. There's no use trying to be nice about it. The kingdom of God has suffered a great deal of harm from fighters—men who would rather fight than pray; but the kingdom of God has also been done great harm by men who would rather be nice than be right. I believe that God wants us to be right, though He wants us to be right lovingly.

The first false worship is Cain worship, which is worship without atonement. This kind of worship rests upon three basic errors. One is the error that assumes God to be different from what He is. He who seeks to worship a God he does not know comes without having first been cleansed by the coals from off the altar. But this kind of worship will not be accepted by God.

The second error is that man assumes he occupies a relation to God that he does not occupy. The man who worships without Christ and without the blood of the Lamb and without forgiveness and without cleansing is assuming too much. He is mistaking error for truth, and spiritual tragedy is the result.

The third error is that sin is made less serious than it is in fact. The psychologists and psychiatrists and sociologists and that gang of left-wingers that have come in during the past years have taken the terror out of sin. To worship God acceptably we must be freed from sin. Cain worship is worship out of an unregenerate heart.

And then there is Samaritan worship. It is heretical worship in the correct meaning of the word *heretical*. Heresy is picking out what you want to believe and rejecting, or at least ignoring, the rest. This the Samaritans did. They worshipped Jehovah, but they didn't worship in Jerusalem; they worshipped at Samaria. The history of the Samaritans shows that there were some Jews among them and that they had Jewish theology. But they had their Jewish theology all mixed up with pagan theology, and it was neither fish nor fowl but an unholy mixture of both. That is Samaritan worship, and our Lord said, "Ye worship ye know not what" (John 4:22).

Then there is nature worship. That is the worship of the natural man, only on a very poetic and philosophical level. It is an appreciation for the poetry of religion. It's a high enjoyment of the contemplation of the sublime. When I was a young fellow and didn't know any better, I studied, more or less for fun, the old-fashioned and now thoroughly repudiated doctrine of phrenology. It says that the shape of your head tells what you are.

There are certain bumps on your head that reveal your personality. If you have a bump here just above your forehead, that's the bump of sublimity. You love the sublime. Such are the poets; they like to look at trees and write sonnets. Well, there's a good deal of religion and supposed worship that is no higher than that. It's simply the enjoyment of nature. People may mistake the rapt feeling they have in the presence of trees and rivers for worship. Ralph Waldo Emerson said that he had at times—on a moonlit night walking across a meadow after a rain and smelling the freshness of the ground and seeing the broken clouds with the moon struggling through—he said he had often been glad to the point of fear. Yet Emerson was not a regenerated man. He did not claim to be.

I want to warn you against the religion that is no more than love, music and poetry. I happen to be somewhat of a fan of good music. I think Beethoven's nine symphonies constitute the greatest body of music ever composed by mortal man. Yet I realize I'm listening to music; I'm not worshipping God necessarily. There's a difference between beautiful sounds beautifully put together and worship. Worship is another matter.

Now, I'm very much concerned that we realize that the worship I'm talking about has a sharp theological definition, that there must be truth in it, that it must lie within the confines of eternal truth or it is rejected.

"God is a Spirit: and they that worship him must worship him in spirit and in truth" (John 4:24). Only the Holy Spirit can enable a fallen man to worship God acceptably. As far as that's concerned, only the Holy Spirit can pray acceptably; only the Holy Spirit can do anything acceptably. My brethren, I don't know your position about the gifts of the Spirit, but I believe that all the gifts of the Spirit not only ought to be but have been present in His church all down the centuries. The Spirit's gifts to the church are the organs through which the Holy Spirit works, and He cannot work through His church without the organs being present. You cannot account for Augustine and Chrysostom and Luther and Charnock and Wesley and Finney except they were men gifted by the Holy Ghost.

I believe that the Holy Spirit distributes His gifts severally as He will to the church and that they are in the church and have been in the church all along. Otherwise the church would have died the day that everybody who had been in the upper chamber died. The church has been propagated by the Holy Spirit, so we can only worship in the Spirit, we can only pray in the Spirit, and we can only preach effectively in the Spirit, and what we do must be done by the power of the Spirit. I believe that the gifts are in the body of Christ and they who worship God must worship Him in the Spirit.

But also we must worship Him in truth. Now the worshipper must submit to truth. I can't worship God acceptably unless I have accepted what God has said about five things. Before my worship is accepted, I must accept what God has said about Himself. We must never edit God. We must never, never apologize for God. No man has any right to get up in the pulpit and try to smooth over or amend anything that God has said about Himself. There is that passage about God hardening Pharaoh's heart. There have been books written to explain that away, but I will not explain it away. I will let it stand. If I don't understand it, I will let it stand anyway. I believe what God says about Himself.

Then to worship correctly I must believe what God says about His Son—not what some philosopher says about God's Son, or some theologian. I must believe what God says about His Son Jesus Christ our Lord. Then I must believe what God says about me. I must believe all the bad God says about me, and I also must believe all the good things He says He'll do for me. I must believe I'm as bad as God says I am, and I must believe His grace is as great as He says it is.

Then I must believe whatever God says about sin. Here's another place where the psychologists and psychiatrists have done us great injury. They have euphonized sin. They call it a guilt complex. I believe that our trouble these days is that we've listened to the blandishments of these children of Adam and that we're afraid to see anybody get on his knees and get really scared.

Some of you have no doubt read of Peter Cartright, the great Methodist preacher who lived a century or so ago. Well, Peter was quite a preacher—an ignorant fellow, but God was on him. They tell how he once went to a conference and preached. The conference was in the charge of a little fellow from a seminary and of course Peter had little time for those boys. When Peter gave the invitation a lot of men came, including a big logger—a great big brawny fellow with monstrous, apelike arms, a huge fellow. He came down to the front and threw himself down and began to pray.

He'd been a sinner and he told God about it loudly, which scared this little seminary student half to death. He ran to him and said, "Compose yourself, brother, compose yourself." Peter Cartright pushed him aside, slapped the big logger on the back and said, "Pray on, brother, there's no composure in hell where you're going." Finally the man saw the goodness of God and the power of the cross, and the grace of God reached down and saved him. He leaped to his feet with a howl of delight and looked around for someone to hug and the first fellow he got hold of was the little seminary student. He picked him up and went dancing around and shouting at the top of his voice. It was hard on the young student's dignity, but perfectly right nevertheless.

Now it is possible to have religious experience without Jesus Christ. It's not only possible to have religious experience, it's possible to have worship without Jesus Christ. That is, it is possible for a man to have an experience of talking with God or being talked to by God. Look at Cain. Cain had a religious experience, but God did not accept him. Look at Balaam, son of Beer. He had an experience and yet God was not pleased with him. In an old Catholic church in Mexico I saw a pale-faced old lady come and kneel down before a statue of the Virgin. With her hands together and her eyes open and her face set in worship she was having a real religious experience, but it was in the presence of the Virgin Mary. In a church in the United States I saw a huge statue of the Virgin, much larger than any person here; her bare feet were extended so the worshippers could kiss them and her great toe on one foot had been worn down with the lips of those who came to worship.

Yes, it's possible to worship but not be accepted by God

Almighty. Brethren, I'm not sure but that those old pagans who believed in the gods of Olympia and Valhalla, who called God Thor or Zeus, were having some kind of an experience; but they died and perished nevertheless. It is not an experience that saves us; it is the blood of the Lord Jesus Christ. Worship is not simply having a solemn feeling about the length of time and the brief duration of our lives on earth and the vastness of the heavens and the smallness of our bodies. That may be beautiful but it's not worship. To worship acceptably, I repeat, is to be born anew by the Holy Ghost through faith in the Lord Jesus Christ and have the Holy Spirit of Christ teach us to worship and enable us to worship.

> We praise Thee, O God, we acknowledge
> Thee to be the Lord.
> All the earth doth worship Thee, the Father
> everlasting.
> To Thee all angels cry aloud, the heavens and all the
> powers therein;
> To Thee Cherubim and Seraphim continually do cry.
> Holy, Holy, Holy, Lord God of Sabaoth;
> Heaven and earth are full of the majesty of Thy glory.
> The glorious company of the Apostles praiseThee.
> The goodly fellowship of the Prophets praise Thee.
> The noble army of Martyrs praise Thee.
> The holy church throughout all the world doth
> acknowledge Thee,
> The Father of an infinite Majesty;
> Thine adorable, true and only Son;
> Also the Holy Ghost, the Comforter.

So says the old Te Deum.

WORSHIP:
THE NORMAL EMPLOYMENT OF MORAL BEINGS

Why did Christ come? Why was He conceived? Why was He born? Why was He crucified? Why did He rise again? Why is He now at the right hand of the Father?

The answer to all these questions is, "In order that He might make worshippers out of rebels; in order that He might restore us again to the place of worship we knew when we were first created."

Now because we were created to worship, worship is the normal employment of moral beings. It's the normal employment, not something stuck on or added, like listening to a concert or admiring flowers. It is something that is built into human nature. Every glimpse of heaven shows them worshipping; Ezekiel 1:1–5, the creatures out of the fire were worshipping God; Isaiah 6:1–6, we see the Lord high and lifted up and hear the creatures saying, "Holy, holy, holy, is the Lord of hosts"; Revelation 4:8–11, God opens heaven and we see them there worshipping God the Father; and in the fifth chapter, verses 6–14, we see them worshipping God the Son.

Worship is a moral imperative. In Luke 19:37–40 the whole multitude of disciples were worshipping the Lord as He came along and some rebuked them. The Lord said, "Don't rebuke them; if they didn't worship Me the stones would cry out."

Now, worship is the missing jewel in modern evangel-icalism. We're organized; we work; we have our agendas. We have almost everything, but there's one thing that the churches, even the gospel churches, do not have: that is the ability to worship. We are not cultivating the art of worship. It's the one shining gem that is lost to the mod-ern church, and I believe that we ought to search for this until we find it.

I think I ought to talk a little more about what worship is and what it would be like if it were in the church. Well, it's an attitude, a state of mind, a sustained act, subject to degrees of perfection and intensity. As soon as He sends the Spirit of His Son into our hearts, we say "Abba" and we're worshipping. That's one thing. But it's quite another thing to be worshippers in the full New Testament sense of the word and up to our possibilities.

Now I say that worship is subject to degrees of per-fection and intensity. There have been those who wor-shipped God to the place where they were in ecstasies of worship. I once saw a man kneel at an altar, taking Com-munion. Suddenly he broke into holy laughter. This man laughed until he wrapped his arms around himself as if he was afraid he would burst just out of sheer delight in the presence of Almighty God. A few times I have seen other people rapt in an ecstasy of worship where they were carried away with it, and I have also heard some simple-hearted new converts saying "Abba Father." So worship is capable of running from the very simple to the most intense and sublime.

Now what are the factors that you will find present in worship? Let me give you a few of them as I go along. First, there is boundless confidence. You cannot worship a Be-ing you cannot trust. Confidence is necessary to respect, and respect is necessary to worship. Worship rises or falls in any church altogether depending upon the attitude we take toward God, whether we see God big or whether we see Him little. Most of us see God too small; our God is too little. David said, "O magnify the Lord with me" (Psalm 34:3), and "magnify" doesn't mean to make God big. You can't make God big. But you can see Him big.

Worship, I say, rises or falls with our concept of God; that is why I do not believe in these half-converted cowboys who call God the Man Upstairs. I do not think they worship at all because their concept of God is unworthy of God and unworthy of them. And if there is one terrible disease in the church of Christ, it is that we do not see God as great as He is. We're too familiar with God.

Communion with God is one thing; familiarity with God is quite another thing. I don't even like (and this may hurt some of your feelings—but they'll heal) to hear God called "You." "You" is a colloquial expression. I can call a man "you," but I ought to call God "Thou" and "Thee." Now I know these are old Elizabethan words, but I also know that there are some things too precious to cast lightly away, and I think that when we talk to God, we ought to use the pure, respectful pronouns.

Also I think we ought not to talk too much about Jesus just as Jesus. I think we ought to remember who He is. "He is thy Lord; and worship thou Him." And though He comes down to the lowest point of our need and makes Himself accessible to us as tenderly as a mother to her child, still don't forget that when John saw Him—that John who had lain on His bosom—when he saw Him, he fell at His feet as dead.

I've heard all kinds of preachers. I've heard the ignorant boasters; I've heard the dull, dry ones; I've heard the eloquent ones; but the ones who have helped me most were the ones who were awestruck in the presence of the God about whom they spoke. They might have a sense of humor, they might be jovial; but when they talked about God, another tone came into their voice altogether; this was something else, something wonderful. I believe we ought to have again the old biblical concept of God that makes God awful and makes men lie facedown and cry, "Holy, holy, holy, Lord God Almighty." That would do more for the church than everything or anything else.

Then there is admiration—that is, appreciation of the excellency of God. Man is better qualified to appreciate God than any other creature because he was made in His image and is the only creature who was. This admiration for God grows and grows until it fills the heart with wonder and delight. "In our astonished reverence we confess Thine uncreated loveliness," said the hymn writer. "In our astonished reverence." The God of the modern evangelical rarely astonishes anybody. He manages to stay pretty much within the constitution. Never breaks over our by-laws. He's a very well-behaved God and very denominational and very much one of us, and we ask Him to help us when we're in trouble and look to Him to watch over us when we're asleep. The God of the modern evangelical isn't a God I could have much respect for. But when the Holy Ghost shows us God as He is, we admire Him to the point of wonder and delight.

Fascination is another element in true worship. To be filled with moral excitement. To be captivated and charmed and entranced. Excited, not with how big you're getting or how big the offering was. Not with how many people came out to church. But entranced with who God is, and struck with astonished wonder at the inconceivable elevation and magnitude and splendor of Almighty God.

I remember as a young Christian when I got my first awful, wonderful, entrancing vision of God. I was in West Virginia in the woods sitting on a log reading the Scriptures along with an old Irish evangelist by the name of Robert J. Cunningham, now long in heaven. I got up and wandered away to have prayer by myself. I had been reading one of the driest passages imaginable from the Scriptures where Israel came out of Egypt and God arranged them into a diamond-shaped camp. He put Levi in the middle and Reuben out in front and Benjamin behind. It was a diamond-shaped moving city with a flame of fire in the middle giving light. Suddenly it broke over me: God is a geometrician; He's an artist! When He laid out that city, He laid it out skillfully, diamond-shaped with a plume in the middle, and it suddenly swept over me like a wave of the sea: how beautiful God is and how artistic and how poetic and how musical, and I worshipped God there under that tree all by myself. You know after that I began to love the old hymns, and I have been a lover of the great hymns ever since.

Next is adoration, to love God with all the power within us. To love God with fear and wonder and yearning and awe. To yearn for God with great yearning, and to love Him to a point where it is both painful and delightful. At times this will lead us to breathless silence. I think that some of the greatest prayer is prayer where you don't say one single word or ask for anything. Now God does answer, and He does give us what we ask for. That's plain; nobody can deny that unless he denies the Scriptures. But that's only one aspect of prayer, and it's not even the important aspect. Sometimes I go to God and say, "God, if

Thou dost never answer another prayer while I live on this earth, I will still worship Thee as long as I live and in the ages to come for what Thou hast done already." God's already put me so far in debt that if I were to live one million millenniums I couldn't pay Him for what He's done for me.

We go to God as we send a boy to the grocery store with a long written list. "God, give me this, give me this, and give me this," and our gracious God often does give us what we want. But I think God is disappointed because we make Him to be no more than a source of what we want. Even our Lord Jesus is presented too often much as "Someone who will meet your need." That's the throbbing heart of modern evangelism. You're in need and Jesus will meet your need. He's the Need-meeter. Well, He is that indeed; but, ah, He's infinitely more than that.

Now when the mental and emotional and spiritual factors that I've spoken to you about are present and, as I've admitted, in varying degrees of intensity, in song, in praise, in prayer and in mental prayer, you are worshipping. Do you know what mental prayer is? I mean by that, do you know what it is to pray continually? Old Brother Lawrence, who wrote *The Practice of the Presence of God*, said, "If I'm washing dishes, I do it to the glory of God and if I pick up a straw from the ground, I do it to the glory of God. I'm in communion with God all the time." He said, "The rules tell me that I have to take time off to go alone to pray, and I do, but such times do not differ any from my regular communion." He had learned the art of fellowship with God, continuous and unbroken.

I am afraid of the pastor who is another man when he enters the pulpit from what he was before. Reverend, you should never think a thought or do a deed or be caught in any situation that you couldn't carry into the pulpit with you without embarrassment. You should never have to be a different man or get a new voice and a new sense of solemnity when you enter the pulpit. You should be able to enter the pulpit with the same spirit and the same sense of reverence that you had just before when you were talking to someone about the common affairs of life. Moses came down from the mount to speak to the people. Woe be to the church when the pastor comes up to the pulpit or comes into the pulpit! He must come down to the pulpit always. Wesley, they said, habitually dwelt with God but came down at times to speak to the people. So should it be with all of us. Amen.

Other Titles by A.W. Tozer

The Attributes of God, Volume I

The Attributes of God, Volume II

The A.W. Tozer Electronic Library, on CD-ROM

The Best of A.W. Tozer, Book One

The Best of A.W. Tozer, Book Two

Born After Midnight

The Christian Book of Mystical Verse

Christ the Eternal Son

The Counselor

The Early Tozer: A Word in Season

Echoes from Eden

Faith Beyond Reason

Gems from Tozer

God Tells the Man Who Cares

God's Pursuit of Man (formerly *Pursuit of Man* and *Divine Conquest*)

How to Be Filled with the Holy Spirit

I Call It Heresy!

I Talk Back to the Devil

Jesus, Author of Our Faith

Jesus Is Victor

Jesus, Our Man in Glory

Let My People Go, A biography of Robert A. Jaffray

Man: The Dwelling Place of God

Men Who Met God

Mornings with Tozer

The Next Chapter After the Last

Of God and Men

Paths to Power

The Price of Neglect

The Pursuit of God

The Pursuit of God: A 31-Day Experience

The Radical Cross

Renewed Day by Day

The Root of the Righteous

Rut, Rot or Revival

The Set of the Sail

The Size of the Soul

Success and the Christian

That Incredible Christian

This World: Playground or Battleground?

Tozer on the Almighty God

Tozer on Christian Leadership

Tozer on the Holy Spirit

Tozer on Worship and Entertainment

Tozer Speaks (in two volumes)

Tozer Speaks to Students

Tozer Topical Reader

Tragedy in the Church: The Missing Gifts

The Warfare of the Spirit

We Travel an Appointed Way

Whatever Happened to Worship?

Who Put Jesus on the Cross?

Wingspread, a biography of A.B. Simpson

The following titles are also available as audio CDs, unabridged editions:

The Attributes of God Volume 1

The Attributes of God Volume 2

God's Pursuit of Man

The Pursuit of God